Turkish Me

Sidney Whitman

Alpha Editions

This edition published in 2024

ISBN : 9789362512642

Design and Setting By
Alpha Editions
www.alphaedis.com
Email - info@alphaedis.com

As per information held with us this book is in Public Domain.
This book is a reproduction of an important historical work. Alpha Editions uses the best technology to reproduce historical work in the same manner it was first published to preserve its original nature. Any marks or number seen are left intentionally to preserve its true form.

Contents

PREFACE ....- 1 -
PART I ....- 3 -
CHAPTER I   INTRODUCTORY ....- 5 -
CHAPTER II   THE ARMENIAN OUTBREAK IN
CONSTANTINOPLE (August 1896)......................................- 10 -
CHAPTER III   THE OUTBREAK OF THE GRÆCO-TURKISH
WAR ....- 24 -
CHAPTER IV   JOURNEY THROUGH ASIATIC TURKEY- 35 -
CHAPTER V   JOURNEY THROUGH ASIATIC
TURKEY: II..- 49 -
CHAPTER VI   JOURNEY THROUGH ASIATIC
TURKEY: III ....- 59 -
CHAPTER VII   SUMMARY OF OUR JOURNEY ....- 68 -
PART II ....- 79 -
CHAPTER VIII   YILDIZ ....- 81 -
CHAPTER IX   SULTAN ABDUL HAMID ....- 93 -
CHAPTER X   A CITY OF DIPLOMATISTS ....- 106 -
CHAPTER XI   THE LEVANTINE..- 114 -
CHAPTER XII   THE TURK AND HIS CREED ....- 120 -
CHAPTER XIII   TURKISH TRAITS ....- 133 -
CHAPTER XIV   TURKISH TRAITS: II ....- 140 -
CHAPTER XV   CONCLUSION ....- 149 -
APPENDIX...- 160 -

PREFACE

Our aim should be neither to mock, to bewail, nor
to denounce men's actions, but to understand them.

SPINOZA

THE following pages are the outcome of several prolonged visits to Constantinople, Macedonia, and Asiatic Turkey, covering a period of twelve years, from 1896 to 1908. Several of these were made under exceptional circumstances and embody experiences such as do not often fall to the lot of a traveller, some of which, I venture to think, are of lasting public interest.

Anyone who has had personal relations with an autocrat—in this case the spiritual head of a faith in which in the course of centuries thousands of millions of human beings have lived and died—ought to have much to tell worth recounting. There were also the surroundings of the Monarch to be observed. Many a trait of deep human interest presented itself to him who was a privileged visitor: for instance, the ups and downs of fortune as they affected the all-powerful favourite whose good offices—as in the time of a Madame de Pompadour—powerful Sovereigns did not think it beneath their dignity to strive and compete for. Such a man I have seen in disgrace, shunned by those who had hitherto prostrated themselves before him. Finally, I have met him in the streets of London, living under an assumed name in fear of assassination.

At one time it has been my lot to sleep on couches covered with the costliest products of the Turkish loom; at another on the bare floor in a dirty wayside han (camel shed), with camels and oxen as bedfellows, typhus and small-pox hovering around us. Hospitality has been extended to me in the underground mud-hut of the fierce, though hospitable, Kurdish chieftain, armed to the teeth, and next morning I have beheld the snow-capped summit of Mount Ararat, peering seventeen thousand feet high through the clouds. I have seen the streets of Constantinople bathed in the sunshine of summer, and a few hours later besmeared with blood. The life of the people has presented itself to me in the workshop of the artisan, with the boatman on the Bosphorus, with the soldier on the march, and I have felt at home in such company. To all this may be added many opportunities of entering into the spirit and thought of a people usually so exclusive that Europeans may live for years in Turkey without ever having an opportunity of gaining the confidence of a single Mohammedan in any walk of life.

Our quick-living age is so full of transient impressions that "to-day" has become the avowed enemy of "yesterday." Men who but recently played a prominent part in the world are forgotten; they are obliged to die in order to reveal the fact that they were until just now still living. If the material of my book is partly concerned with the things of yesterday, the incidents and characters which it displays may at least claim to illustrate a series of abiding human truths.

If it is only now, after a lapse of years, that I have decided to issue these fragments of my memories, the delay is due to the fact that as long as the ex-Sultan was on the throne my personal relations with him and with those around him formed an obstacle which seemed to check my pen. My narrative might perhaps have been discounted under the suspicion that it was influenced by undue partiality or tainted by motives of self-interest. Now that things have so completely changed there can be but little danger of such an interpretation of my motives.

In describing certain traits of Turkish character I have intentionally dwelt by preference on those which are brightest, because prejudice and detraction have created an impression which calls for a correction of values. My book, therefore, does not lay claim to judicial impartiality. My aim has been to show by a recital of actual experiences that the Mohammedan Turk, whose religion is that of sixty millions of British subjects, is far better than his repute. I have written in frank sympathy with his sterling human qualities, and with a keen sense of the injustice he has long suffered from Christian opinion in Europe.

The Governor of Constantinople one day in 1896 said to me: "England was for us once a garden full of roses, a subject of pleasant thought, sight, and memory. Now, alas! a serpent has entered and brought discord between us."

In the course of my work a trifling incident led me into a correspondence with the late Professor Arminius Vambéry, whose letters, full of insight into Turkish affairs and goodwill towards England, will be found reprinted in the [Appendix](). I am also indebted to my friend Lieutenant-Colonel H. P. Picot, who was H.B.M.'s Military Attaché in Teheran from 1893–1900, for a short contribution which will likewise be found in the Appendix, p. [294]().

From many mementoes in my possession I have chosen the autographed portrait of Ghazi Osman Pasha for reproduction as being that of the hero of a people whose fine qualities no one who is acquainted with them can fail to admire.

S. W.

PART I

CHAPTER I

INTRODUCTORY

Not oft I've seen such sight nor heard such song,
As wooed the eye, and thrilled the Bosphorus along.

BYRON, Childe Harold, Canto xi.

IN the spring of 1896, at a time when public attention centred on the Armenian troubles, the Sultan of Turkey sent a confidential emissary to London for the purpose of sounding the Marquis of Salisbury on the situation without the knowledge of the Turkish Ambassador. He endeavoured to obtain an interview with the Prime Minister, but without success. The Turkish Ambassador was anything but pleased at this Palace manœuvre, and did his best to prevent his master's agent being received. Costaki Pasha, with whom I was on friendly terms, told me that it was bad enough to be kept waiting for one's salary, but it was adding insult to injury to have your position undermined by unauthorized missions.

The Sultan's emissary informed me during his stay that the Sultan was most anxious to ascertain Prince Bismarck's opinion on the Armenian question, and if possible to learn what the Prince would advise him to do in reference to the embarrassing situation in Crete, and he begged me to assist him in this matter.

Shortly afterwards I paid a visit to Prince Bismarck at Friedrichsruh (June 26, 1896). After referring to the action of the Greek Committees which were fomenting trouble throughout the Levant, the Prince expressed his disapproval of the fire-eating Greek Press and the folly of its European backers, who, as he asserted, were at the bottom of the whole disturbance. It was on this occasion that the Prince, in answer to a question, made the since oft-quoted sarcastic remark that "he took less interest in the island of Crete than in a molehill in his own garden." Referring to the Sultan and his troubles, Bismarck put his hands up to his ears, extending the open palms outwards, so as to imitate the attitude of a hare and to convey the idea of the Sultan's timidity in face of a situation which called for exceptional nerve and strength of purpose.

On my return to London in the beginning of July, I received a request from the proprietor of the *New York Herald* to come to Paris. On my arrival he asked me whether I would be willing to go to Constantinople to represent his paper there for a couple of months. Sixteen years previously I had visited

Turkey as a tourist, and I thought I should like to see the country again. So I accepted the offer on the spot.

We owe to a popular writer the assertion that there is something fundamentally different in character between the East and the West, which makes mutual understanding difficult and assimilation impossible. The English traveller who is inclined to accept this axiom may begin to detect the Eastern flavour of things as soon as he leaves the frontier of the German Empire behind him and passes through the Austro-Hungarian Monarchy on his way to Constantinople. Monarchs and statesmen may come and go, laws may be promulgated and the ballot-box may be adopted, but the character of a people is not materially changed even by such measures as compulsory education and universal military service. The East has adopted some of the machinery of Western life, but the Eastern remains an Eastern still. Institutions unsuited to a people's traditions and character may only jeopardize its fortunes:

A thousand years scarce serve to form a State,

An hour may lay it in the dust: and when

Can man its shattered splendour renovate,

Recall its virtues back, and vanquish Time and Fate?

Childe Harold, Canto xi, stanza lxxxiv.

Should you arrive at Vienna on a Saturday, you will have to wait there twenty-four hours if you intend to take the Orient Express to Constantinople, for it leaves Vienna on Sunday evening, and even in that short time you may feel a subtle change in the atmosphere of life. You ask a sedate-looking official in the bureau of your hotel up to what o'clock on Sunday morning the shops in the town remain open, as you want to purchase a few travelling necessaries. "Till mid-day, sir," is the decisive reply. Instinctively warned by past experience, you turn to the hallporter, who usually embodies the brain power of a Viennese hotel, and in order to make sure you put the same question to him. "The shops are not open at all, sir, on Sundays," is his reply: and so indeed it turns out to be.

You stroll towards the Leopoldstadt with the intention of taking lunch at the old "Goldener Lamm," now called the Hotel National, long renowned as the hostelry patronized by European crowned heads as far back as the Vienna Congress in 1815. You grip the brass handle of a glass door on which the inviting word "Entrée" is affixed in large white enamelled letters. You tug at it in vain and are ultimately warned off by a man signalling frantically from the inside that it is not a door at all, but only the window of an apartment—

and that the real entrance to the Hôtel is a few yards to the left. You now recollect that when you were there last—some seven years previously—that blessed word "Entrée" was already there, and that you—and doubtless many others ever since—were warned off, the proprietor not having deemed it worth while to do away with the misleading letters.

It is still Sunday, and you wish to post a registered letter. This can only be done at the Central Post Office during certain hours of the afternoon. You drive there, holding your letter in readiness, together with a "krone" to pay the registration fee, and wait your turn patiently. For without patience, that supposed Christian virtue (which, by the way, I subsequently acquired myself and discovered to be of Mohammedan origin), it is of little use starting on a journey to the East. At last your turn comes and you patiently watch the registering clerk, after slowly copying the address of your letter into a book, retire to the back of his capacious office. You notice that he is engaged in earnest consultation with a colleague. At last, he comes forward with an air of embarrassment and explains apologetically that he is in a "difficulty" as to providing the change out of the small coin you have handed him. Finally, he asks whether you would mind accepting a postage stamp of the value of ten heller (one penny) in part discharge of the sum due to you.

All this happens within twenty-four hours! You know now that you are well on your way to the East, where a minimum value of time and an element of fiction mixed up with every action or statement of fact constitute two of the many differences between the easy-going East and the matter-of-fact West. But there are compensations in the altered aspect of life, and one is the deep impression which Constantinople produces on the stranger by its gorgeous variety of colouring, its movement, and its polyglot chaos.

Constantinople with its five hundred gardens and palaces, its six hundred and eighty mosques, minarets, and towers rising above the sea in the form of a huge amphitheatre, offers to the eye a truly fascinating panorama. Byron extolled its position as incomparable to anything he had ever seen. That great traveller and student of nature, Alexander von Humboldt, thought Salzburg, Naples, and Constantinople the three most beautiful sites in the world. Such is its mysterious charm that "a Sea of Impressions stirs the soul—as a balmy breeze plays gently upon a cornfield in bloom. An intoxicating aroma is wafted towards us. All the wonders of the Eastern World seem to float before our vision—fables and palaces of the Arabian Nights."

But if Constantinople must ever possess an attraction for the traveller by virtue of its unique situation, a deeper interest lies in its unrivalled historical associations, covering two thousand five hundred years of the world's history. From the days of Darius, Alcibiades, and Justinian—when the corn-laden galleys from the Black Sea glided swiftly past the shore opposite Seraglio Point—down to the present time, Constantinople has always been the object of desire of ambitious rulers of nations.

Seen on a summer morning from a window on the upper floor of the Pera Palace Hotel, the city presents a dazzling picture of kaleidoscopic beauty. We are several hundred feet above the level of the sea. It is early morn, and a thick grey fog conceals the waters of the Golden Horn as well as the land. Gradually, as if awakening from a dream, the sharp angles of prominent buildings, the tips of tall minarets, the curved outlines of stately mosques, emerge through the mist between clusters of dark cypresses, dotted in stray patches away to the horizon. The rays of the rising sun strike a few windows here and there. These glisten with a peculiar iridescence, as if lighted by electricity—peeping through the impenetrable haze still dimming the ground. Something ghost-like pervades the scene. Fancy conjures up the vain anger of Polyphemus, the deriding jeers of Ulysses.

Rooks caw overhead as they circle through the air. Chanticleer crows on a patch of green meadow-land. Dogs bark with unwonted anger as three bears, led by their keepers, thread their way through the crowd—well accustomed to such sights. Resounding above all, the trumpet call from the Cavalry Barracks vibrates, mingling with the shouts of hawkers in the street. Fog-horns and the siren's moan from ships at anchor swell the chorus, and between whiles the tinkling of bells of passing mules and horses is distinctly heard. Droves of black sheep, followed by Thracian shepherds in picturesque garb, and numbers of horses of Anatolian breed, ridden by barefooted boys, pass by. Amid this pandemonium, bricklayers are at work on the roof of a seven-storied building, run up in such primitive fashion that you wonder the whole structure does not collapse and bury them among its wreckage. Yet cobblers and tailors are unconcernedly plying their craft in the basement, completing a picture which, if witnessed on the stage or described in a story-book, would strike us as a fanciful realization of a mythical world.

But lo! the sun! Mosques, minarets, and cypresses float out of the grey mist as it lifts slowly off land and water. Turkish ironclads become substantial things as they lie at anchor in the Golden Horn alongside the battered old wooden hulks of Navarino's bloody memory. At first the iron prows only are visible, tipped with light. But as the sun grows more powerful and plays on the water, streaks of silver quiver serpent-like—a veritable Greek fire—round the hulls, until finally the ironclads themselves appear majestically before the vision like antediluvian monsters.

An old disused Turkish cemetery is spread out in front of us with its mournful grove of cypresses. Not so very long ago the whole space from the Hôtel down to the water's edge was one huge graveyard containing the dead of centuries. Théophile Gautier tells us that the Turk loves to be near his dead. To-day only a stray gravestone is left here and there to mark the resting-place of some pious personage hallowed for his faith, his virtues, and on no account to be desecrated by the removal of his bones. Farther away is the suburb of Cassim Pasha, on its fringe the Marine Ministry, and close by, on a hill, the Marine Hospital. Adjoining this, still farther to the right, is the Ters Hanè, the Turkish Government dry-dock on the banks of the Golden Horn. And if the eye takes a wider sweep to the right, the asylum of the poor, Fakir Hanè, comes into view—a noble structure beautifully situated, handsomely endowed by Sultan Abdul Hamid, and, with true Turkish charity, devoted to the poor of all creeds alike. Then there are the Cavalry Barracks, the Greek High School, the so-called Phanar—another instance of Abdul Hamid's munificence. Finally, as we survey the scene from left to right, the cupolas and minarets of five different mosques, each erected in honour of some noted Sultan—Bajezid, Suleiman, Schah-Zadè, Mahmud, Selim—come into the picture and crown the horizon.

This, in faint outline, is the panorama of life and colour which, once witnessed, is stamped for all time on the memory. Yet the imagination is, perhaps, even more deeply stirred by the same scene deprived of its cacophonic noise and its bright colouring in the mysterious stillness of a summer night.[1] Thousands of twinkling lights tell of the unchecked life of the city. The starlit heavens speak a language of their own. They whisper of the transitoriness, the vanity, the futility of what the human heart clings to, and, as if to emphasize the sadness of it all, the twang of a harp and a guitar breaks the silence. The dulcet accents of a woman's voice—a Mignon of this Eastern land—ring out to their accompaniment. The musicians are gipsies—that mysterious race of nomads, wanderers like ourselves towards a distant bourne.

> [1]. On great occasions, such as the Sultan's birthday, the contrast of day and night is still further heightened by the illumination of the warships in the Golden Horn and other craft in the Bosphorus.

CHAPTER II

THE ARMENIAN OUTBREAK IN CONSTANTINOPLE (August 1896)

There is no sure foundation set in blood;
No certain life achieved by other's death.

SHAKESPEARE, *King John*

MUCH that I shall have to say in the course of the next few chapters might be unintelligible, or at least liable to be misunderstood, if I were not to explain the circumstances under which I went to Constantinople as Correspondent of the *New York Herald*. My visit was, as indicated in the previous chapter, in direct connexion with the so-called "Armenian Atrocities," and my mission was due to the shrewdness of one man, a great newspaper proprietor.

For some time past the diplomatic and consular representatives of the Powers at Constantinople had sent alarming reports to their respective Governments, and these, passing into the Press, and supplemented by harrowing accounts from the foreign newspaper correspondents in Constantinople, had fanned a flame of resentment directed against the Turks as Mohammedans. This was more particularly the case in England and the United States of America.[2] The proprietor of the *New York Herald*, almost alone among newspaper magnates, had the discernment to perceive that the Armenian question was in the main a political one—in some respects similar to that of Bulgaria a generation previously—and that whatever might be the shortcomings of the Turkish Government and its local Administration, there was little or no reason for assuming that the disturbances had their source in religious fanaticism directed against the Christian as such; whilst evidence was accumulating that a vast Armenian conspiracy, nurtured in Russia and encouraged by the Nonconformist element in England, obscured the real issue, to which there were two sides. Mr. Gordon Bennett saw the chance of a journalistic "score" in giving the Turks an opportunity of making their own version of things known to the world—a chance which had been denied to them by the great English newspapers.

[2]. See English Blue Books for the years 1895–1896.

This was my first experience as a Special Correspondent abroad, and before starting, Mr. Gordon Bennett had given me his ideas of the duties of such as follows: "The Special Correspondent of a great newspaper possesses for the time being something of the influence of an Ambassador from one nation to another. Now, according to an axiom of Machiavelli, an Ambassador should endeavour to make himself *persona grata* with those to whom he is accredited, if only thereby to gain the best opportunities for obtaining every possible information and to be able to report events in a broad impartial spirit. The correspondent should give his sources wherever possible, and allow the reader to form his own opinion on the facts submitted. The views of the paper itself should be found in the editorial columns. The correspondent is to take no side, and to express no opinions of his own. In many cases it would appear that the matter sent to the papers by their correspondents in Turkey is biased against the Turks. This implies an injustice against which even a criminal on trial is protected."

Having stated this much, I may add that it would be an error to suppose that it was expected of me to palliate or gloss over the gravity of any excesses which might have taken place, for such would only have frustrated the object in view. As a matter of fact, no foreign correspondent in Constantinople gave more unvarnished accounts than those published by the *New York Herald* of the terrible events which subsequently took place in the Turkish capital.

One of the salient features of Constantinople is the prevalence of idle gossip, and I had not been there many days before I became aware that my presence and its supposed purpose formed a topic of interest to people whose very existence was unknown to me. One day, entering the Club de Constantinople, near the Pera Palace Hotel, I was addressed in English by a fat, sallow-faced, beardless individual, who told me with the blandest of smiles that he had heard I had come to Constantinople to "write up the Turks," and that I was to be paid neither more nor less than one million francs to do so. He asked me quite ingenuously whether this was indeed the case.

With such an auspicious opening it could not be a matter for surprise that before long the *Herald* correspondent became an object of curiosity to the large colony of "gobe-mouches" who supplied current gossip in the guise of personal news to Embassies and newspaper correspondents.

A conviction had gained ground in diplomatic circles, intensified by the Press in general, that the Turkish Government was, if not actually unwilling, at all events unable to prevent the recurrence of massacres. The agitation on the part of the Armenian Committees in the different capitals of Europe had been carried on to such purpose that there was hardly an American or English newspaper which had a good word left to say of the Turks, let alone of the Turkish Government. A horde of adventurers of various nationalities, déclassés of every sphere of life, cashiered officers among the rest, who had left their native country for its good, were eking out a precarious livelihood by providing newspaper correspondents, if not also Embassies, with backstair information. Others were in the pay of the Sultan or his chamberlains, at the same time acting as spies, watching and reporting the doings of people of note in the capital in the interests of the Palace.

Thus whenever a stray communication, signed with some pseudonym, appeared in a newspaper, it was at once assumed that it emanated from a tainted source. For such was the prejudiced state of Anglo-Saxon feeling against the Turks at this particular period—much to the delight of England's rivals on the spot—that it was quite sufficient to be known as a philo-Turk to be credited with some kind of rascality.

My letters of introduction opened all doors to me, so that, had there been any news to get hold of, I was favourably placed to obtain it, more particularly from official Turkish sources. I was, therefore, much disappointed at the meagre information procurable, either at the Sublime Porte or at the Palace itself, since I had openly stated that my one desire was to be put in a position to get hold of important items of news, if possible earlier than my competitors, and to give the Turkish side, or version, of events as they took place. This was the only favour asked, and I was extremely surprised at the helplessness of the Turks to avail themselves of a powerful organ of publicity ready to give them fair play. Instead of meeting me in a sensible spirit, one of the first things the Turkish authorities did was to confiscate the *New York Herald*. Mr. Whittaker, the *Times* correspondent, whom I informed of what had taken place, said: "They are hopelessly dense. Tell them that if they want the truth told they must let a correspondent manage things in his own way." But this the authorities were either disinclined to do or incapable of doing all the time I was in Constantinople. Thus almost every bit of news I obtained came to me independently of Turkish sources, and was the result of my own individual efforts. Powerlessness on the part of the official Turks to avail themselves of an influential journal anxious to show them to the world in their true colours (surrounded by enemies and slanderers as they were on all sides, in the face of a serious crisis) was confessed to me one day in pathetic terms by Mehmet Izzet Bey, one of the Sultan's translators, in the words: "Mon cher, nous sommes un peuple taciturne; nous ne savons pas nous défendre."

I had been some weeks in Constantinople, and there was no sign of anything unusual being about to happen; nothing which would have justified me in continuing to idle away my time in that city. So I wrote to Mr. Bennett asking him to allow me to return home. But, as it soon became apparent, this was only the lull before the storm. On the afternoon of August 26, a Mr. Whittall, an English resident, volunteered to accompany me on a shopping expedition to the Bazaar in Stamboul. We took the funicular tunnel railway from Pera down to Galata, but had no sooner alighted at the latter station than we were witnesses of an extraordinary scene.

Everybody was in a state of wildest excitement. We were hustled out of the station, the iron gates of which were immediately shut, turning us, as it were, into the street, where on all sides the iron shutters of the shops were being hastily put up with a deafening din. Every door was closed against us, and we just managed to find shelter on some steps leading down into a cellar so as to survey the scene. All this happened with incredible rapidity. Simultaneously, a shrieking and gesticulating savage crowd, of the type seen unloading ships in the harbour, came along from the left, surging on towards the Galata Bridge. They were armed with what, as far as I could make out, were wooden laths, such as might have been split off from cases, or legs wrenched off tables and chairs, and were in hot pursuit of a couple of Armenians who, covered with blood, were running immediately in front of them, evidently flying for life. They passed so rapidly that it was difficult to distinguish between the pursued and the pursuers. The rattle of musketry was incessant; it played an accompaniment to the dramatic scene, and seemed to be coming from the vicinity of the Ottoman Bank, into which, as we only heard later in the day, a band of Armenian revolutionists had forced an entry, overpowered the personnel in charge, barricaded the doors, and begun throwing bombs and firing revolver shots out of the windows on to the crowd in the street.

Led by curiosity and the natural desire of a correspondent to see what was going on, we crept along, skirting the side of the houses in the direction of the firing, until we reached the corner of a narrow street leading up to the Ottoman Bank. From here we saw some Turkish soldiers standing in front of the Bank building and firing in the direction of the windows, from which came shots in return. Half-way between them and where we stood we could distinguish a number of dead bodies on the ground.

On our way up the hill, back to the hotel, we passed several more dead lying either in the road or in the side streets. Nobody came near them, as would have been the case in many European countries; no curiosity was shown: they lay prone as if death had been the result of some sudden cataclysm, or shock, which had subsided as suddenly as it came.

The pavement as well as the middle of the streets showed big patches of blood, proving that the massacres, which apparently had started among the harbour population of Galata and Stamboul, had spread to the heights of Pera. I took a walk through the Grande Rue de Pera and the adjoining thoroughfares, in which every shop was closed, but did not meet a soul. Had it not been for the dogs, which struck me as being unusually depressed, Constantinople might have been a deserted city, and this state of things lasted for several days. Such was the tension of nerves that when I returned to the hotel I found the messenger boy who had shown me the way to the telegraph office near the British Embassy, and whom I had subsequently lost sight of, in tears. He had spread the report that I had been murdered. As a matter of fact no Europeans ran any appreciable risk of harm during those days, except, perhaps, through the accident of an Armenian bomb exploding in the street in their immediate vicinity. At night a table was placed in the hall of the hotel, on which were placed a number of revolvers, so that each guest might take one up to his room, and have a weapon with which to defend himself. But for the dull thud of the bekdji's (night watch) wooden staff striking the pavement an uncanny stillness prevailed, as of a dead city. During that night and the subsequent ones the dead were taken in carts past our hotel and hastily interred in the Armenian cemetery on the way to Tschishly.

Early next morning I went out with the correspondent of the *Times*. We visited the Ottoman Bank, from whence the Armenian conspirators had, only a few hours before, been taken away. Everything was in the greatest disorder. Pools of blood on the first floor and in the basement remained as evidence of what had taken place during the previous twenty-four hours. We were shown a heap of blood-stained coins. On the second floor we saw a table still littered with the remnants of the last meal of the Armenians. The staff of the Bank had escaped through the roof when the Armenians made their attack.

We thence wended our way to the Galata Bridge, upon which dense crowds had congregated, the Turkish guard being doubled at the head of the bridge, the wooden planks of which were dotted with a spray of blood spots. In the afternoon a friend took me to a house near the Galata Tower. We climbed up to the roof, from which we obtained a bird's-eye view of the harbour, and saw a crowd rushing from all directions towards the quay—apparently on the alert to renew the outbreak.

I went up to the Palace in the afternoon and found everybody in a state of great excitement. There could be no doubt of the helplessness of the authorities in the face of the action of the mob; but great stress was laid on the provocation given by the Armenian conspirators, which nobody could have foreseen and which the Armenian Patriarch Osmanian had publicly repudiated and denounced. The Turkish officials were indignant that it should be said the movement was inspired by hatred of the Christians as such, and the Sultan's second secretary proceeded to draw up a list for my information of the large number of Armenians who occupied some of the best paid Ministerial posts and were among the Sultan's own staff of Court officials. The list I was assured ran to about twenty per cent. of the higher employees at Constantinople. The Keeper of the Sultan's Civil List—Ohannes Effendi—was an Armenian, as was also the chief Censor of the Press.

Next morning I went by steamer to Buyukdere to see the Russian Ambassador, M. de Nelidow, who, through his chief dragoman, M. Maximow, had negotiated the escape of the Armenian bank-breakers. M. Maximow had gone up to the Palace, and by his language, the like of which had never been heard in the decorous precincts, frightened the Palace officials. There was some talk at the time of the British Fleet being ordered up to Constantinople, a rumour which I mentioned to the Russian Ambassador. It did not appear to please him, for he exclaimed rather excitedly: "Oh, par exemple! Nous ne rendrons jamais la clef de notre maison"—a remark the significance of which has never been absent from my thoughts from that day to this in connexion with Turkey and her future.

I then called on Abraham Pasha at his summer residence, also at Buyukdere. I had made his acquaintance a few weeks previously at the Sultan's Palace, and had been his guest at the Cercle d'Orient. A great landowner and sportsman, as I could see the trophies in the hall of his palatial konak, he was reputed to be the wealthiest and most influential Armenian notability in Turkey, and had always been on the very best terms with Abdul Hamid. He had even had the honour of entertaining his predecessor, Abdul Aziz, at his country seat. I found him in bed, guarded by a body of armed retainers, in a state of great trepidation. "What is this? What is it all coming to? It is really too bad!" he ejaculated as I was ushered into his bedroom. As a matter of fact Armenians had been killed at Buyukdere. So great was the terror among the Armenians of position that one of the wealthiest, the banker Azarian, to whom I had brought a letter of introduction from the London house of Rothschild, closed his place of business and fled to the Prinkipo Islands. It was a novel sensation to see millionaires, thus exposed to the slings and arrows of outrageous fortune, being pursued like rats, and if caught knocked on the head as little better than vermin.

The most extraordinary feature of this popular rising against the Armenians, at least from an ethnological point of view, was the discrimination exercised by the mob in seeking their victims. Thus, to a stranger, it would be often difficult enough to distinguish between an Armenian and a Greek, an Italian, or a Jew, at least by the cast of his features; and among Armenians there are Protestants, Roman Catholics, and Orthodox Greek Churchmen. Yet those who belonged to the Orthodox Greek Church, and were thus supposed to be implicated in the revolutionary propaganda fomented in Russia, were sought out and hounded to death. Hardly any Roman Catholic Armenians were molested, for they were reported to have refrained from revolutionary activity. How the unlettered crowd of Kurds, Lazis, and other Turkish tribes constituting the lower classes of Galata were able to exercise such discrimination still remains a mystery to me.

In the midst of the massacres going on in broad daylight a Jewish moneychanger in one of the streets of Galata was assailed by a crowd and was on the point of being felled to the ground. In his abject terror the man called out: "For God's sake, let me go! I am not an Armenian; I am a Hebrew." The mob, though in a frenzy of passionate excitement, desisted for a moment, and the man's assertion proving to be true, the crowd released him. The terror-stricken wretch rushed away, leaving the contents of his stall, a mass of gold and silver coins, strewn on the pavement. Several Turks forming part of the murderous crowd pursued him, crying out: "Come back and pick up your money; we don't want to rob you."

It is only fair to state that the German colony stood practically alone in not succumbing to the prevailing panic. Even on the 26th of August, when, in the first hours of consternation, public offices of every other nationality were closed, the German Post Office, which is situated close to the Ottoman Bank—in the very centre of the disturbance—remained open and sent off its post-bags as usual. Bearing the German flag aloft, the officials took the sacks of letters over the Galata Bridge to the railway station in Stamboul, where the massacres were at their height. I mention this fact, even after this lapse of time, because the cool-headedness of the Germans on this occasion was one of the contributory causes which, from that time onwards, made them rise in the favour of the Sultan and the officials at the Palace at the expense of the influence of other nationalities, who, for the time being, had apparently lost all sense of proportion. This incident derives its significance not so much from the presence of mind which the Germans displayed as from the fact that it showed that they alone, among the foreign element, were conversant with the political nature of this outbreak, and refused to believe and to be influenced by its supposed religious origin. The Germans knew that as Christians or foreigners they had nothing to fear, whereas the agitation carried on in England by Canon McColl and the Duke of Westminster, backed by sundry fervent Nonconformists, had had the effect of exhibiting the fanatical Turk as thirsting for the blood of the Christian. Thus, when the crisis came, those who had allowed their minds to be dominated by these personages failed to show that calmness and self-possession which are otherwise marked characteristics of the English race when suddenly assailed by peril.

Only a few English families, such as the Whittalls, merchant princes who have lived in Smyrna and Constantinople for generations, and whose name is a household word among the Turks, did not lose their heads. They even exercised their influence to afford shelter to the Armenians whose lives were in danger.

Through a mere chance, brought about, moreover, by my ignorance of the conditions of the Press censorship prevailing at the time at Constantinople,

I was enabled to secure a "score" for the *New York Herald*. For twenty-four hours that paper was the only one in the outside world which had the news of the Armenian attack on the Ottoman Bank and the massacres in Constantinople which were its immediate sequel. This came about as follows: Foreign newspaper correspondents in Constantinople, aware by experience of the difficulties put in their way by the censorship when forwarding news unfavourable to the authorities, were in the habit of sending their contributions by post to Philippopolis, the Bulgarian frontier town, where each of them kept a running account at the post office. From thence their communications were forwarded by telegraph to their destination; a procedure which, for newspaper purposes, involved a loss of twenty-four hours. This I was unaware of, and thus ingenuously sent my telegram direct from Constantinople to Paris, where it arrived the same evening, its contents appearing in Paris and New York the next morning, before the same item of news had even reached Philippopolis. It was afterwards stated that this priority was due to favouritism granted me as correspondent of the *New York Herald*; but this was not the case. It was simply an oversight on the part of the Press censor, probably due to the extraordinary excitement prevailing generally in Constantinople at the time. In proof of this, I may mention that the telegram I sent off the next day was stopped; indeed, it did not reach its destination at all, and the one I sent on the day after arrived in Paris containing the obviously exaggerated statement that twenty thousand Armenians had been massacred. Any favouritism I was credited with must in this last case have led to the publication of a piece of news very damaging to the Turks. Most of the other assertions made about that time respecting my activity as representative of the *New York Herald* had no better foundation in fact. The story that the Press censor had been discharged for stopping one of my telegrams was as baseless as the rest. As a matter of fact he retained his post until his death, and when I was last in Constantinople, in 1908, his son, also an Armenian, had been appointed his successor.

One day, immediately following upon the attack on the Ottoman Bank, the police discovered a large quantity of explosive bombs of different sizes in the cellar of a house in Pera, which, it was said, had been brought there with Russian connivance. Now, although the correspondents of the different European papers were invited to inspect the find, which was afterwards publicly exhibited at the Arsenal (Tophanè), such was the general disinclination to admit any fact which could tell in favour of the great provocation the Turks had received from the Armenian revolutionists that hardly any publicity was given to this discovery of bombs.

One morning during the Armenian disturbances a card was brought to me bearing the name of his Excellency Ahmed Midhat Effendi, Vice-Président du Bureau Impérial de Santé Publique (Sanitary Administration of the Ottoman Empire).

A tall, broad-shouldered, black-bearded man, in the prime of life, of imposing bearing and with flashing dark eyes, wearing the fez and dressed in the conventional black coat of high Turkish officials, termed Stambolin, without any decoration, gold braid, or other indication of his status, was shown in. He told me that he had come on the part of his Imperial Majesty the Sultan to place himself at my disposal, in case I should require his services, either to give me introductions, or to serve me as guide and interpreter, as he possessed a perfect command of the French language. He said the Sultan had read several of my communications to the *New York Herald*, and was pleased that there had come to Constantinople a correspondent who was ready and able to make allowances for the great provocation the Turkish authorities had received from the Armenian revolutionaries, and to treat Turkish affairs from an impartial standpoint.

As this gentleman will be mentioned several times in the course of these pages—for to my subsequent relations with him I am indebted for much of my insight into the Turkish character—a few words concerning him may not be out of place. The story of his early life and of his subsequent relations with Sultan Abdul Hamid is an interesting one, and calculated to throw a sympathetic light on the character of the Sovereign. Born of humble parents in the Island of Rhodes, his father was either a dealer in cloth, or, like President Andrew Johnson, a tailor; and he himself was apprenticed to the calling. Being, however, imbued with a taste for literature, Ahmed Midhat went into journalism and subsequently politics. Here he came into contact with the Young Turkish Movement of Midhat Pasha, and became implicated in the movement which led to the impeachment of that statesman in 1877. One day the Sultan sent for Ahmed Midhat, as he afterwards told me, and quite charmed him by his gracious manner, turning him from an opponent to a champion, convinced that his master's one aim was the good of his country, so that he finally burst forth with the declaration that the Sultan could reckon on him as one of his devoted slaves. "I do not want you as a slave; I ask you to be my friend," the Sultan replied, finally captivating the generous-minded, confiding man. Ahmed Midhat thus became an ardent and sincerely convinced adherent of the Hamidian régime, and from all accounts he was one of the few who never turned their influence to unworthy ends. His position as part proprietor of the *Terdjumani Hakkikat*, a Turkish newspaper, secured him independence. In his spare time he turned to literature, and eventually became known and honoured throughout the Turkish Empire as a regenerator of the Turkish language. He had been to Paris, where he made the acquaintance of Victor Hugo and other literary notabilities, and several of his novels—of an almost childlike simplicity of thought—were translated into French and German. When I made his acquaintance he was the virtual head of the administration of public health, and one of the very few Turks who were given a private seal, which assured that whatever communication he might wish to make to the Sultan would immediately reach His Majesty. In spite of all these advantages Midhat was hardly ever to be met at the Palace. His private life was in harmony with his public conduct. He lived with his family in his own konak at Beikos, on the Bosphorus, not far from the Black Sea, under plain but patriarchal conditions, and there I was his guest on several occasions. He had two wives and sixteen children, six of whom were Christians he had taken into his family because they were poor and destitute and had brought up as his own. I asked him how he came to take such a course, and why he had not preferred to adopt Mohammedans. "They were my neighbours," he said. "They were poor and had nobody to look after them, and I do not believe in proselytism. They are good and grateful; that is sufficient."

I paid repeated visits to different Turkish mosques on the Mohammedan Sunday (our Friday). There had been statements in English newspapers referring to the Sultan's unpopularity, and I discussed these with Ahmed Midhat. He said the suggestion that the Sultan had no following was not true, but I might easily convince myself, as there was no surer indication of the people's feeling on this point than the popular attendance at the mosques. During the last months of Abdul Aziz's reign the mosques had been quite deserted, for the people were disgusted with a Sultan-fainéant—a drone who only lived for self-indulgence; whereas the present Sultan was venerated as a Sultan—"travailleur qui travaillait jour et nuit pour le bonheur de son peuple. In spite of the disastrous war of 1877, and even of these latest disturbances, the Sultan was beloved by his people." In every case I found the mighty Aja Sophia in Stamboul crowded with worshippers; all classes mixed up promiscuously, the pasha kneeling next the Hamal, the common soldier beside the field-officer. An atmosphere of earnest devotional fervour pervaded the scene. Its sincerity was emphasized by children unconcernedly playing about the recesses of the building, and sundry old men—to all appearances beggars or cranks—moving along the aisle in and out of the kneeling crowd, unmolested. Looking up to the mosaic inlaid dome of the building, the outline of the figure of Christ was distinctly visible through the covering of whitewash, paint, or gilt which had in all probability been laid over it after the taking of Constantinople, when the Christians made their last stand in this very building.

In order to prove to me how baseless were the fables regarding the Mohammedan desecration of Christian churches, Ahmed Midhat drove me some days later to the Kariè mosque, where the fresco figures of the saints of the Byzantine church, though somewhat dilapidated, were still plainly recognizable on the walls.

Shortly after the news had spread to Europe of the attack on the Ottoman Bank and the subsequent massacre of Armenians, a number of artists of illustrated newspapers arrived in Constantinople, commissioned to supply the demand for atrocities of the Million-headed Tyrant. Among these was the late Mr. Melton Prior, the renowned war correspondent. He was a man of a strenuous and determined temperament, one not accustomed to be the sport of circumstances, but to rise superior to them. Whether he was called upon to take part in a forced march or to face a mad Mullah, he invariably held his own and came off victorious. But in this particular case, as he confided to me, he was in an awkward predicament. The public at home had heard of nameless atrocities, and was anxious to receive pictorial representations of these. The difficulty was how to supply them with what they wanted, as the dead Armenians had been buried and no women or children had suffered hurt, and no Armenian church had been desecrated. As an old admirer of the Turks and as an honest man, he declined to invent what he had not witnessed. But others were not equally scrupulous. I subsequently saw an Italian illustrated paper containing harrowing pictures of women and children being massacred in a church.

The weeks following the outbreak of the Armenian conspiracy were of a somewhat trying nature. It was long before things regained their normal character. The clang of the closing of the iron shutters of the shops reacted on the nervous system of the inhabitants of Pera for years. Even after twelve years Turkish soldiers, who were ordered to patrol the streets of Pera after the massacres, were still to be seen in the Grande Rue de Pera at night doing the same drudgery.

In the course of my journalistic work I had occasion to visit the Gumysch Soujou Hospital, situated near the German Embassy. About forty Turkish soldiers were lying there, wounded by Armenian bombs or revolver shots during the street fighting. I wrote an article dealing with this subject and a description of the wounded, which must have been of a sympathetic character, for it was subsequently translated and reproduced in the Turkish newspapers. I was told that it had attracted the notice of the Sultan and that he would like to see me before I left Constantinople; but weeks passed by and I heard no more of the matter. It was the second week in October, and I was about to return home.

I was on the point of leaving Constantinople when a messenger from the Palace brought me word that Izzet Bey, the Sultan's second secretary, wanted to see me at once. On arriving at the Palace he came towards me, smiling, with the words: "Sa Majesté vous offre un dîner and wishes to see you before you leave Constantinople." I returned to the hotel in order to don evening dress for the occasion, and on coming back to the Palace at about seven o'clock in the evening, I was ushered into a room in the centre of which stood a table already set for dinner, which was served and cooked in French style in contradistinction to the usual mode of the Palace. Wines of various kinds, including champagne, were handed round, presumably for my sole benefit, since the other guests only drank water. This gave the entertainment a somewhat incomplete character. After dinner Izzet Bey took me aside, and again expatiated on the great services I was supposed to have rendered to his country. "Mon cher, un milliard ne pourrait pas vous recompenser pour ce que vous avez fait pour nous," were his words. I was then, and am still, conscious only of having acted in a fair and sympathetic spirit where others had persistently given a one-sided account of events. I replied to that effect, adding that as correspondent of the *Herald* I could not think of accepting any remuncration from anybody. Izzet Bey continued that the Sultan wanted to know something about my position in life, as he took an interest in me and would like me to come to Constantinople permanently and enter his service in a suitable capacity. He then asked me to follow him, as the Sultan would like to see me at once. It was about nine o'clock in the evening when we wended our way towards the one-storied villa-like white stucco structure where the Sultan habitually received visitors. We passed through a glass door into a spacious hall, in which stood groups of tall men clad in black frock-coats cut close up to the neck in Turkish fashion, and wearing fezes. These were apparently the Sultan's body-servants. What struck me more particularly was that they wore no uniform or any insignia of office or distinctive mark, or bore any arms. Indeed, there was not a single armed or uniformed person about; a plain civilian attire was evidently *de rigueur* in the immediate vicinity of the Sovereign. There was something distinctly impressive in this simplicity. It suggested a striking contrast to the glittering pomp and circumstance surrounding some other monarchs. I still recall the deferential attitude of this little knot of Imperial servants towards the humble mortal who for the moment was lifted upon a pinnacle of earthly distinction by the desire of the Padishah to shake hands with him. My position reminded me of the French Ambassador who told the Russian Emperor Paul that an important personage in his empire took a great interest in a certain matter, whereupon the autocrat interrupted him sharply with the words: "There is nobody of importance in my empire except the man with whom I am now conversing, and only as long as I speak to him is he important."

But an autocrat must not be kept waiting beyond the bare second which is required to leave one's goloshes outside the door. This done, we passed through to the right into a brilliantly illuminated apartment, the floor of which was covered with a costly Turkish carpet; the chime of a beautiful grandfather clock heralded our arrival. The Sultan came towards me as I entered the room, shook hands, and led the way to a sofa, in front of which stood a small tabouret with coffee-cups and some cigarettes. Two gilt chairs were placed opposite the sofa, apparently for the occasion—to which he motioned us—whilst he himself sat down on the sofa and handed me a cigarette. He faced us resting both his hands on the hilt of his sword—for he was clad in the uniform of a Turkish General—with the Star of the Order of Imtiaz in brilliants suspended from his neck. I noticed then, as on subsequent occasions, that the Sultan wore a single ring. It was a large emerald. So much has been written in depreciation of this extraordinary man that I cannot resist the temptation of reiterating the impression of kindliness and sincerity which he made on me. In saying this I make all allowance for our common human weakness in crediting those of exalted station who are kind to us with every virtue, whilst viewing askance others who neglect us. But the fact remains that Abdul Hamid, without any physical advantage to speak of—rather the reverse, for the features and figure might without much imagination have been supposed to belong to a Galata money-changer—possessed an exceptional charm of manner, a simple dignity and grace of bearing, which were calculated to, and indeed did, gain the sympathies of those who were brought into contact with him. There was something in his look and in the even-toned balance of his sympathetic voice when addressing his secretary which betrayed the habit of command, the exaction of implicit, even slavish, obedience during a lifetime. It interested me to note the attitude of extreme deference of those surrounding him. Thus Izzet Bey only sat on the extreme edge of his chair with his hands crossed flat on his chest and his head bent low while the Sultan told him in Turkish what he desired should be communicated to me. The Sultan wished to thank me for the sympathetic manner in which I had written on Turkish subjects, and expressed his gratitude that for once a journalist had come to Constantinople apparently free from those prejudices against the Turks which were a source of so much trouble and annoyance to him.

Rightly or wrongly, the Sultan seemed to think that he was under a personal obligation to me which he did not deem sufficiently liquidated by the bestowal of decorative distinctions. He suggested that I should leave the *New York Herald*, come to Constantinople, and enter his service. He wished me to remain attached to his person in some capacity or other. I replied that I could not see my way to enter his service, as it seemed to me that he had already too many people round him who drew big salaries for doing little or nothing, and that at my time of life I had no desire to come to Constantinople and live there. I added that wherever I might happen to be I should always take pleasure in endeavouring to secure fair play for Turkey and her ruler—a promise I have since faithfully kept.

"Well then," rejoined the Sultan, smiling good-humouredly, "if you will not enter my service, come and see me again as a friend and be my guest whenever you return to Constantinople; I shall always be glad to see you."

Knowing that I was about to leave Constantinople and that I was personally acquainted with Prince Bismarck, His Majesty asked me to take a case of china ornaments—a pair of vases and a painted plaque—from the Imperial porcelain factory as a present from him to the Prince. The Sultan desired me to assure the Prince of his friendly regard and to tell him that he hoped he would always exercise his great influence in favour of Turkey, a country to which Moltke, his illustrious countryman, had in days gone by rendered valuable service. This commission I subsequently carried out on my way home through Germany.

When I left the Sultan and walked out into the open air, into the balmy calm of a starlit autumn evening, not a soul was to be seen. The splashing of water from a fountain which issued from a wall on the left was the only break of silence around, except the sound of our feet as they pressed the loose gravel. Nor did I meet a guard or soldier or any living soul as I passed the porter's lodge out of the Palace. As far as I could tell there would have been nothing to prevent a determined band of half a dozen armed men from entering the Palace and kidnapping the Sultan there and then, as others had entered the Ottoman Bank, the porters of which, in their picturesque Albanian costume, were armed to the teeth.

I left Constantinople the next day, the 12th of October.

CHAPTER III

THE OUTBREAK OF THE GRÆCO-TURKISH WAR

Beauteous Greece,

Torn from her joys, in vain with languid arm

Half raised her lusty shield.

Dyer

IN the winter of 1896–97 I had been acting as Special Correspondent for the *New York Herald* in Vienna, when, towards the end of February, things began to wear a sinister aspect between Turkey and Greece. Thus I left for Salonica on March 8, in order to await there the development of events. On that day Greece finally declined to accede to the demand of the Great Powers to recall Colonel Vassos from Crete. Thereupon Turkey began to mobilize her forces, and to push them forward towards the southern frontier of Thessaly. It was only subsequently, when Greece had also concentrated nearly all her forces on her northern frontier, and Greek volunteers, armed by the Ethnike Hetairia,[3] together with Greek regular troops, repeatedly made incursions into Macedonia, that Turkey declared war. Even then, however, there were hopes of peace left, for Turkey was still inclined to listen to the urgent request of the Great Powers not to assume the offensive.

> 3. A secret Greek political organization with Pan-Hellenistic aims to the activity of which the disturbances in Crete and the outbreak of the Græco-Turkish war were partly due.

At Salonica I had a dull time, living in a state of suspense, with nothing to do but read the newspapers at the Club on the quay, or gaze at the snow-capped crest of Mount Olympus across the bay. A few warships appeared now and then in the offing. The largest ironclad of the Italian navy, the *Duilio*, anchored in front of the city, and it was a treat to visit it and to note the spick-and-span efficiency of the ship.

Rumours of the wildest kind from all manner of unreliable sources—mostly of Greek origin—reached us daily. They tended to show that whatever might be the forces at the disposal of the Turks, Ananias with his hosts was on the side of the Greeks. His artillery was firing its missiles, and these travelled with incredible velocity to the ends of the earth. We learnt from more reliable sources, however, of raids over the frontier undertaken by the Greek Ethnike Hetairia, with whom were the Greek regulars, and who were reported to have committed various acts of pillage and murder, even in the neighbourhood of Salonica, whose Greek population made no secret of its sympathies with the Greek cause. It was not safe to go about after dark, although one felt inclined to risk much to partake of the decently cooked food and that collective social and convivial life which the Germans—here, as elsewhere in Turkey—maintained in the Kegel Club at the Hôtel Colombo.

The Jewish element of Salonica accounts for nearly half the total population, and affords interest to the student of race and character. These Hebrews are in strong contrast with their co-religionists elsewhere, especially in Russia; not only as regards status, but also in appearance. They are fine, strong, handsome men and women. Jews are met with in almost every sphere of life—more particularly among the artisans and the working classes; nearly all the Salonica boatmen are Jews. Some of the Salonica Jews rise to high positions in different branches of the Turkish Administration and invariably give satisfaction. They are "très bien vus par les Turcs," as a high Turkish official told me; for the Turks, in spite of their supposed fanaticism, have always treated the Jews with kindness, and this at a period when Christian Spain burned them at the stake. I was told that the Jews of Salonica had only recently celebrated the four-hundredth anniversary of their arrival in Turkey from Spain, from which country they were banished in 1490. On this occasion they had sent an address to the Sultan expressing their grateful attachment to Turkey and her Sovereign. Prayers were offered up in every synagogue of the Turkish Empire, and £T50,000 was collected for benevolent purposes under the auspices of a Committee presided over by the Grand Rabbi.

It was at Salonica that I first came into contact with that survival of the fierce spirit of proselytism of former ages, the Anglo-Saxon missionary element. Never do I remember to have met such implacable hatred for the Mohammedans as that which seemed to animate the wife of the Anglo-Saxon missionary, bent on converting them, together with the Jews, to the religion of Love. She set me thinking whether she and her husband might not have been more profitably engaged in the slums of the great cities at home than among the industrious and sober population of Salonica. An honest, hard-working Christian missionary who is kind-hearted and humane in a Mohammedan sense may still do good work in that part of the world, let alone in Asiatic Turkey, as I subsequently convinced myself, particularly in the application of hygiene, since this and medical science particularly are lamentably backward. But only harm can come from the spirit of hatred which I now saw manifested for the first time.

An English working-man of an ill-conditioned type was staying at my hotel. I used to meet him in the café sipping his tea, with an unsightly mongrel dog as his companion. He told me he had come from Lancashire, and was engaged as foreman at some textile works situated on the quay. He had also been in the United States. I asked him how he liked America. He flared up and, pointing to his dog, replied: "You see that ere little *dorg*! Well, I'd rather see 'im dead than in America," bringing his clenched fist down on the marble table with savage emphasis. This was significant, but not the only testimony since vouchsafed to me of the antagonism between the British trade-union spirit and the conditions of labour in the United States.

There was an English public-house in Salonica, on the quay, facing the harbour. It was kept by an English widow, but only opened its shutters on the rare occasions when the English squadrons put into the bay, when it did a brisk business.

One continuous stream of Turkish troops from Albania and Asia Minor passed through Salonica, arriving by sea, and, for the most part, disembarking in the dead of the night. I was often awakened by the dull, plaintive chant of these wild children of Asia, or of the untamed sons of the Albanian hills in their white skull-caps, whose voices mingled with the sounds of the waves beating against the stone quay, along which they marched on their way to the railway station.

I had been in Salonica about ten days when I received a telegram from Mr. Bennett asking me to proceed to the Turkish headquarters at Elassona, not as War Correspondent, for which vocation at my time of life I scarcely felt fitted, but to report on the real state of affairs, concerning which so many rumours were afloat.

I called on the Vali, who gave me the necessary permit and deputed a Circassian officer named Mehmet to be my escort. I engaged a Roumanian, one Hermann Chary, who had formerly been in the service of General Gordon in Egypt, and, I believe, in India as well. He had since drifted to Salonica, and was commissionaire at the Hôtel Impérial on the quay, where I was staying. Even now I often call this man to mind when I read in our newspapers of the extraordinary linguistic accomplishments of some of our leading statesmen who speak French with a Parisian accent or are wonderful German "scholars." Here was a man who spoke some nine or ten languages fluently, but had to be content to earn five francs a day as interpreter in a third-rate hotel, and was delighted with the chance I offered him of better employment. He accompanied me later in the same capacity on my journey through Armenia.

We left Salonica on March 20—a Saturday—and our departure for Elassona was marked by the following childlike flourish of trumpets in the *Journal de Salonique* (March 22):

"Mr. Sidney Whitman, Correspondent of the *New York Herald*, left our city last Saturday for Elassona in order to follow the operations of the troops. The local authorities of Sorovitch have gracefully placed a military escort at the disposal of the American journalist, which will accompany him to the frontier.

"Mr. Whitman is one of those rare correspondents of foreign newspapers who have appreciated without malevolence the attitude of the Imperial Ottoman Government in the various incidents which have happened of recent years.

"We may be sure that again to-day he will keep the innumerable readers of the *New York Herald* correctly informed as regards the imposing military forces of Turkey, the admirable discipline of her troops, their valour, their bravery, and their irreproachable conduct. The American paper has sent another correspondent to the Greek Camp, and a third one to Constantinople. It is always by telegraph that these gentlemen communicate with their paper. One can thus form an idea of the enormous expenditure which the *New York Herald* incurs in order to justify its reputation as the best and most promptly informed journal."

We proceeded by rail to Karaferia, which left us about eighty miles to Elassona by road, and took the road to Sorovitch, where we spent the night as guests of a pasha and reached our destination in the evening of the next day. As we came nearer to Elassona we passed a large number of troops on the road, for they were all converging towards that point, not merely from Salonica, but also from the port of Katerina, where 1200 horses and mules were disembarked daily by army contractors. Many of the men we saw were cavalry, clad in the most fantastic style. Some of them rode mules, and, in addition to a belt full of cartridges round their waist and shoulders, carried a pickaxe, a knife, charcoal for lighting a fire, and a supply of flour, sugar, rice, barley, and beans. Their foot-covering was the so-called "Tcharik," consisting of a piece of untanned leather tied with string to the ankle and leg. The villages we passed through offered next to no accommodation; swallows built their nests in the dilapidated tenements. In this truly desolate and wholly uncultivated country it was difficult to imagine it had ever formed part of the dominions of Philip and Alexander of Macedonia. But what its economic possibilities might become under reasonable conditions was brought home to us when our energetic interpreter provided a large glass bottle of excellent red wine, holding a full gallon, which, bottle and all, he had purchased in the village of Kossona for thirteen pence in English money!

The *Herald* at that time was regarded by the Turks as one of the few foreign newspapers ready to give them fair play, and this ensured me a kindly welcome from everybody—from the generalissimo of the Turkish forces, Edhem Pasha, down to the humblest subaltern.

Elassona is a town of about four thousand inhabitants, situated on the banks of the River Xerias, on the western slope of Mount Olympus, and is supposed to be identical with the Oloosson mentioned by Homer.

Quarters were assigned to me, my interpreter, and the Circassian officer, Mehmet, in the house of the mayor of the town, which had been vacated. All the rooms were left empty but for a bare couch or two. Nor did I see anybody in the house during my stay except now and then a stray devout Mohammedan kneeling on a carpet in one of the rooms, solitary and silent, engaged in prayer.

Edhem Pasha, who received me shortly after my arrival, was still in the prime of life, and looked what he was, a fine representative of the high-bred Turk. He was simple, courteous, benevolent, and endowed with that innate dignity which Orientals seem capable of uniting even with humble station. I must assume that a favourable report had preceded us, for he welcomed me at our first meeting in his konak, attended by some officers of his staff, almost as a friend, playing with his "tisbe" between his fingers while he talked. Throughout my stay of eight days he continued to show me every kindness in his power. He even consented to be photographed at my request, with one of his officers on either side of him. This was the photograph which afterwards made the round of the illustrated newspapers of the world; for I never met with any other, the high-class Turk rarely posing before the camera. But with all his amiability there was a deal of punctilio about the Turkish Commander-in-Chief. He could be inexorable at times. Later, when war was declared and a host of correspondents appeared on the scene, some of these gentlemen arrayed themselves in military uniform. Edhem Pasha promptly informed them that, although they might possibly be entitled to wear such costume in their own country, they were only accredited to him as newspaper correspondents, and as such would not be allowed to appear in uniform.

Fifty-five thousand Turkish soldiers were said to be quartered in and around that primitive old town. Not a single woman was to be seen; not a drop of wine or spirits could be procured for love or money. We were told that twenty years before, during the Russo-Turkish war, twenty-four thousand Turkish soldiers died here of typhus and dysentery.

Riding towards the camp, we met soldiers everywhere, some of them leisurely sitting by the roadside cooking their meals. As we rode past them an aide-de-camp of the Sultan turned to me and, pointing to the Albanian Redifs, said: "These fellows know no greater delight than that of being called upon to fight, and, if needs be, to die for the Sultan."

One afternoon I rode out, accompanied by Mehmet Tscherkess, a young Turkish major who had served in the Prussian Guards, and who was, besides, an aide-de-camp of the Sultan and my interpreter to the Meluna Pass, which formed the frontier towards Greece at that particular point. When the war broke out three weeks later some fierce fighting took place here. A small block-house on a summit marked the Turkish boundary-line, and a couple of hundred yards away a similar structure denoted the Greek border, where we could discern a group of Greek soldiers. The Sultan's aide-de-camp suggested that I should walk over and have a talk with the Greeks; which I did, accompanied by my dragoman. We were met half way by a Greek cavalry officer. He told us that he had been trained at the French cavalry school of Saumur, and in manner and conversation he certainly reminded us more of a Frenchman than a Greek. To a casual remark of mine he replied light-heartedly—even truculently—that war was inevitable, as also was the defeat of the Turks! Looking down into the valley, the far-famed vale of Tempè lay before us, through which Pompey rode a fugitive, flying from the fateful field of Pharsalia. We could just perceive Larissa in the distance. The little white tents of the Greek forces lay spread out at our feet and were plainly visible amid a landscape more advanced in the verdure of spring and bearing far more signs of cultivation and closer habitation than that we had passed through in Macedonia. We parted on good terms. I rejoined the Turkish officers, and rode leisurely back to Elassona.

On leaving Elassona the Turkish Commander-in-Chief had prepared a little surprise for us. We started on horseback at about five o'clock in the morning, as it was reckoned that it would take all day to do the forty miles to Katerina, on the coast. After riding for about an hour, and turning a sharp angle of the road, we beheld a squadron of Turkish cavalry drawn up at the salute to bid the representatives of the *New York Herald* a parting good-bye. Even to-day I cannot think of this little incident without the reflection how grateful the Turks were for the smallest proof of fairness towards them, and how rarely they got it. We rode on leisurely all day, and so scorching was the sun, although we were only in March, that when I rose next morning in the little Greek inn at Katerina I found the skin had peeled off my ears on to the pillow. From Katerina a Turkish Government torpedo-boat brought us back to Salonica.

War had not yet broken out, but every indication of its inevitability was about us. The hotels were crowded with war correspondents, who had arrived from all parts and were feverishly active, getting ready to proceed to join the Turkish forces, buying horses, prancing about, testing their purchases in the street in front of the hotel, engaging servants, and laying in a stock of provisions. The English public-house I have mentioned did a brisk trade. Among the necessities of the situation was that of obtaining permission from the authorities to be allowed to proceed to Headquarters. Nor was this an easy matter for the representatives of those papers which for years past had relentlessly vilified the Hamidian régime.

One day Mr. J. P. Blunt, the British Consul-General at Salonica, a strong philo-Turk, said to me at the Club: "I want to introduce you to the correspondent of the *Times*." "I am sorry," I replied jokingly, "but I have made it a rule never to allow myself to be introduced to any countryman of mine on the Continent." Experience had taught me, as it must have taught others, that—speaking of the type of Englishmen one is likely to come across on the Continent—if they are in what, according to their lights, is a superior position to your own, they do not desire to make your acquaintance. If, on the other hand, they want something from you, or their status is inferior to yours, it is for them to be introduced to you. Mr. Blunt smiled good-humouredly and added that the *Times* correspondent, who had just arrived from London, had heard of my good relations with the Turkish authorities, and would be very glad if I could afford him some assistance, as he intended to proceed to Elassona the very next morning.

This being the case, I declared my readiness to assist him to the best of my ability. Mr. Blunt thereupon brought Mr. Bigham to my hotel. He was a son of the present Lord Mersey, and impressed me as possessing an equipment which would carry him far under modern conditions of getting on in the world—a view which, I am glad to say, has since been borne out. He wielded a ready journalistic pen, spoke and read Turkish, drank tea and mineral waters, and was evidently as hard as nails. He also wrote a book on his experiences as a war correspondent in the campaign, and very kindly sent me a copy of it after the war was over. I gave him a letter of introduction to Edhem Pasha, allowed my Roumanian interpreter to accompany him, and finally prevailed upon the Governor-General of Salonica to permit the Circassian officer, Mehmet, who had been my companion, to serve as his escort on his journey. The result was that Mr. Bigham arrived at the Turkish Headquarters well in advance of all the other correspondents at that time in Salonica, including that redoubtable but genial philo-Turk, the late Sir Ellis Ashmead-Bartlett.

The Græco-Turkish war afforded what will probably be the last opportunity, at least in Europe, for a fair heyday outing to those belonging to what G. B. Shaw might well have described as, next to that of royalty, "a decaying industry"—the profession of war correspondent.

Among other arrivals at Salonica were several German officers in the Turkish service, notably the late Grumbkow Pasha, on their way from Constantinople to the front. They appeared more eager for the fray than the Turks themselves, like Sir Walter Scott's

Great Chatham with his sabre drawn

Stood waiting for Sir Richard Strachan;

Sir Richard, longing to be at 'em,

Stood waiting for the Earl of Chatham.

This eagerness for bloodshed on the part of men whose country was at peace with the Greeks made a disagreeable impression upon my mind. I was therefore not sorry when a few days later I heard that they had been summoned back to Constantinople, the Russian Ambassador having protested against foreigners in the Turkish service being allowed to fight in the cause of the Infidel against the Orthodox Greek Hellenes.

On April 17—it was a Sunday—war was formally declared, and the Greek flag was hauled down from the Greek Consulate. The streets were crowded with people of every creed and nationality as they would be on a holiday. The day is fixed on my memory by the absence of every vestige of rowdyism, such as might well have been anticipated from the fact that Salonica contained a large Greek population who had never made a secret of their sympathies with their countrymen. I had repeatedly witnessed the small Greek shopkeepers eagerly scanning the Greek newspapers for the latest news, and this in the presence of their Turkish customers without the latter taking the slightest notice. When the flag was taken down from the Greek Consulate it was as if an immense load of uncertainty was lifted from the minds of all. Now at least people knew where they were, and both Greeks and Turks seemed to enjoy the end of the long period of uncertainty.

I left Salonica for Constantinople on the steamer *Policevera* on April 19 in the queerest company, for the vessel carried sixteen hundred sheep and only one passenger—myself. At times my travelling companions tried to prevent me from getting on deck, for they filled the whole of the deck and pressed against the cabin door.

In Constantinople there was outwardly little evidence of the country being at war. The only unusual feature was the crowd of Greeks that blocked the entry to the French Embassy, which had undertaken their protection whilst the war lasted. I remained nearly a month in the Turkish capital, during which not a single instance of offence or personal violence to the Greek population came to my knowledge, although the modern Greeks are among the most demonstrative of races, and are not accustomed to put a curb on their feelings in Turkey.

One evening a dense crowd gathered at the railway station and awaited for hours the departure of the train which was to take Ghazi Osman Pasha to the seat of war. His arrival from the Palace, where he was said to be in close consultation with the Sultan, was expected every minute. At last the carriage of the national hero of Turkey drew up. There was no cheering or shouting of any kind such as would have been the case in some countries—a solemn, almost a mournful silence prevailed. The waiting-room and all the roads leading to the railway station were crowded with Turks, but no "Hurrah!" or "Down with the Greeks!" was heard. Many were engaged in earnest prayer, which they read aloud from little books. Children were lifted up for the venerable warrior to kiss, and old white-bearded men shed tears as Osman kissed their children. It was a touching sight.

One day the Sultan sent me word that he would like me to visit the hospital for the wounded—it was temporarily fitted up in the grounds of the Palace. Marshal Shefket Pasha, the commander of Yildiz, together with two Turkish surgeons, one a pasha, was deputed to accompany me. The wounded were constantly arriving from the seat of war, and were lodged in airy ground-floor sheds, and obviously had every care. I could see by the elaborate surgical appliances and the scrupulous cleanliness everywhere that the operation-rooms, painted white, excluded every particle of dust. They were treated according to the latest scientific principles, and down to the common soldier they had everything that money and goodwill could provide. There was no complaining: Turkish and European doctors vied with each other in caring for the wounded. Several German surgeons had come expressly for the purpose, and had given their services gratuitously. How highly the Sultan appreciated this spontaneous action of strangers is, I think, shown by the fact that he bestowed the Gold Imtiaz Medal, one of the highest Turkish distinctions, which was only given by the Sultan for special services rendered him personally, and which many much-decorated pashas did not possess, on these foreign surgeons.

The Sultan next expressed a wish that I might inspect the "Bazar de Secours" started by him to raise funds for the invalids and the families of the victims of the war. It was a large one-storied building which had been specially erected at his expense a short distance from the Palace, and which was to be opened in a few days to the public. We are sometimes able to estimate the taste, and even the very character, of the inmates of a house by the articles it contains. So also on this occasion the collection of heterogeneous objects exhibited for sale spoke a language of its own. To begin with, almost every third article, and these the most costly, was a gift from the Sultan himself; many others were from members of his household and the fine old Turkish families generally. This war, in which the Christian Greek had hounded the public opinion of Europe against the Mohammedan Turk, deeply stirred the feelings of the Turkish people; and when the news of repeated victories came to hand, the Sultan may be said to have stood on the pinnacle of his popularity. Also, the invitation to contribute to the bazaar met with a ready response from the Turkish upper classes. The ladies of the harem, the wife of the Khedive of Egypt, of the Sheikh ul Islam, and of nearly all the pashas in the capital sent valuable presents. The donations included beautiful old swords, daggers, and yatagans inlaid with precious stones; gorgeous silver-gilt saddle harness, horse trappings, gold boxes and caskets inlaid with precious stones; Gobelins, priceless old embroideries and shawls, gold-framed looking-glasses, and trinkets came from the ladies of the harem. Even a copy of the Koran, bound in leather and ornamented with brilliants, in a gold box inlaid with pearls, was among the collection of gifts. The Emperor of Austria sent a Louis XV cabinet. The German Emperor, the Sultan's friend, sent some samples of the Berlin china works; but more interesting than these were about a dozen prints of Professor Knackfuss's well-known composition, inspired by His Majesty and with an inscription in his own handwriting: "People of Europe, protect your holiest possessions." Each of these costly works of art bore the autographed Imperial signature R.I., and were to be offered for sale to the public for the benefit of the wounded. Alas! no purchasers were tempted; for when I came again to Constantinople I was told that the Sultan himself had bought and paid a fancy price for the lot— for the benefit of the wounded.

Poor Abdul Hamid! Here in this bazaar were childlike faith and genuine human nature to be seen in close propinquity with cheap, hollow unreality: the latter soon to be exposed to the world in its true colours.

Among the many notabilities who were brought to Constantinople by the events of the war was General Nelson Miles, the Commander-in-Chief of the United States Army, whose acquaintance I had the privilege of making. I also met Sir Ellis Ashmead-Bartlett, on his return from the seat of war, flushed with victory; for, as already mentioned, he was an ardent pro-Turk. He was most indignant at the action of the Ambassadors of the Great Powers, who, headed by Sir Philip Currie, had made a protest to the Porte against the "atrocities" alleged to have been committed by the Turkish soldiery in Thessaly. He related how the English newspaper correspondents who were with the Turks as well as he himself felt their sense of fair play outraged by these false charges, and how they had drawn up a report and sent it by telegram from Thessaly to the British Ambassador at Constantinople. He gave me a copy, of which I append a translation; for even at this distance of time—in the winter of Turkish sorrow and misfortune—it is of interest, as affording strong testimony in favour of the much maligned Turkish soldier.

To His Excellency, The Ambassador of Great Britain, Constantinople.

"We are able to give personal testimony to the admirable conduct of the Ottoman soldier as well as the constant and most successful efforts of the Turkish officers to prevent pillage and to protect the Christian inhabitants in every way. The Greeks, who are returning to their homesteads in very great numbers, declared themselves very satisfied with their treatment. The Greek inhabitants of the surrounding villages have sent deputations to solicit the protection of the Turkish troops.

"After the departure of the Greek military authorities from Larissa the Greek Governor liberated the prisoners from the penitentiary and provided them with rifles. These latter, together with other lawless elements, did a deal of damage and pillage at Larissa during the twenty-four hours which elapsed before the arrival of the Turkish troops. The truth of this statement is confirmed by the Greek inhabitants, as also by the Greek priests.

"Only one Greek village, Deliler, has been partially burnt, and this was due to the obstinate fight last Friday in the place itself. Several houses have been demolished here and there from whence shots had been fired on the Turkish soldiery. But the discipline and conduct of the Turkish Army have been admirable, and can be most favourably compared with that of the best troops of the world. All the Europeans with the Army are of this opinion.

"*Signed by*:

E. Ashmead-Bartlett, M.P.; Clive Bigham, Correspondent of the *Times*; Geo. R. Montgomery, Correspondent of the *Standard*; W. Peel, Special Correspondent of the *Daily Telegraph*; H. A. Gwynne, Special Correspondent of *Reuter*'s Agency; G. W. Steevens, Correspondent of the *Daily Mail*; Hamilton Weldon, Special Correspondent of the *Morning Post*."

Before leaving Constantinople I received an invitation from Sir Philip and Lady Currie to a garden party in the beautiful grounds of the British Embassy overlooking the Golden Horn. On such occasions politics were taboo. Everybody who was anybody was present, and a more charming host and hostess it would be difficult to imagine than the British Ambassador and Lady Currie; both since, alas! gone from hence. Among the guests was an old Englishman, once, as I was told, the gardener of the British Embassy in Lord Stratford de Redcliffe's time, and whose son is now one of the most prosperous English traders of Constantinople.

CHAPTER IV

JOURNEY THROUGH ASIATIC TURKEY

The Pontic Sea,

Whose icy current and compulsive course

Ne'er feels retiring ebb, but keeps due on

To the Propontic and the Hellespont.

SHAKESPEARE, Othello

IN the beginning of September 1897 I was taking a "rest cure" at Marienbad when I received a telegram from the proprietor of the *New York Herald* asking me to join him on his yacht *Namouma* at Venice. On my arrival he informed me that he had been to Constantinople and had an interview with the Sultan. In the course of it he had suggested to His Majesty that he should send an expedition into Armenia to verify the facts connected with the disturbances of the last two years, and allow the *New York Herald* to be represented on the occasion.

The Sultan was favourably disposed to the idea, and proposed that I should be the person selected to accompany the expedition. To this Mr. Bennett had, as he told me, demurred; not that he had any reason to doubt my reliability, but the fact remained that it was already known in America that I had had personal relations with the Sultan. This in itself would make it desirable that somebody else should report on this particular subject. It was finally agreed with the Sultan that a member of the New York staff of the paper, the late Dr. George H. Hepworth, should be the correspondent, the Sultan making his final consent dependent upon my accompanying the expedition as well.

Mr. Bennett continued that he had long desired to place his readers in a position to judge things for themselves from information gathered on the spot, and that this matter was one of exceptional interest to the American public, owing to the fact that the Sultan had hitherto declined to allow any newspaper correspondent whatsoever to traverse Armenia, let alone to offer facilities for so doing.

"You will render the *Herald* a great service in accompanying the expedition," he added, "for unless you go it will not start."

It is not often that any man has an opportunity of visiting an unknown country and at one and the same time of obliging an autocratic ruler and a great newspaper proprietor. I therefore accepted Mr. Bennett's suggestion, it being distinctly understood that I was to hold what in legal language is termed a "watching brief" on behalf of the Turks, and that I should not be called upon to write at all unless a controversy arose. In such a case, Mr. Bennett said that Dr. Hepworth and I could fight it out in the columns of the *Herald*, which would act as impartial bottle-holder. Fortunately the necessity did not arise to submit to such an ordeal. The last words Mr. Bennett said to me on leaving were: "In this matter you can look upon yourself as the Sultan's man." And here I may add that, being firmly convinced injustice had been done to the Turks, at least as regards the imputing to them of religious persecution, I willingly undertook the task offered me of seeing "fair play" given to them.

Some weeks elapsed before Dr. Hepworth came from New York and reached Paris, from whence we started together for Constantinople. On our way we broke our journey at Vienna. In travelling on to Belgrade we gave up our sleeping berths to the King of Servia and his father, ex-King Milan, who both travelled by our train, the Orient express. On our arrival at the Servian capital early next morning we witnessed their official reception at the station by the authorities, who looked very much like a gathering of peasants at a country fair. King Alexander did not present a sympathetic appearance; but there was a touch of human nature in the expression of poor Milan which enlisted our sympathy.

We arrived in Constantinople about the middle of October, and encountered at the outset the dilatory tactics which marked the execution of every project emanating directly from his temporizing Majesty. This seemed to depress Dr. Hepworth very much; but as I had known cases of Turkish Ambassadors being kept dawdling about Constantinople for months after they had been appointed to their post, the delay did not surprise me. When, however, one week succeeded another without any decisive step being taken, or any date being appointed for our departure from Constantinople, we were driven to the conclusion that there must be some special cause for the delay. This proved to be the case. Information had reached the Sultan that Dr. Hepworth was really an American clergyman with a strong bias in favour of the missionary element, that he had contributed articles to the *Herald* fiercely condemning the Turkish Government for its treatment of the Armenians, and that he had written editorial sermons for that paper regularly every Sunday for many years past. Under these circumstances the Sultan hesitated to place it within his power to enter Armenia. Such was the information vouchsafed to me by a secretary of the Sultan, accompanied by a request that I should come up to the Palace and have an interview with His Majesty.

Munir Pasha, the Grand Master of Ceremonies, was present as interpreter on the occasion, and in the course of the audience confirmed what I have just stated. I could not deny that Dr. Hepworth, though a journalist by profession, had in early years been a clergyman, and that he still wrote short sermons in the form of editorials in the Sunday number of the *New York Herald*. For all this, I assured the Sultan that, though Dr. Hepworth's sympathies were undoubtedly with the Armenians, this did not necessarily imply unfairness of mind; whereas, if the information to be obtained in Anatolia should turn out to be of a nature to exculpate the Turkish authorities from complicity in what had taken place, Dr. Hepworth, as an honest man, would report accordingly. The very fact of his known sympathy with the Armenians would then double the weight of his testimony. I succeeded in convincing the Sultan; he even agreed that our route should take any direction Dr. Hepworth might decide upon. Nothing was to be hidden or disguised from us, and in case of any difficulty arising I was always to be at liberty to telegraph directly to His Majesty without let or hindrance on the part of the officials accompanying the expedition. The Sultan concluded: "You have already given me substantial proof of your impartiality. Render me this service, and I will grant you any favour you like to ask of me."

To this I impulsively replied, somewhat quixotically as it strikes me to-day, that he might rely on me doing my best in the interests of truth and justice without any consideration of reward entering into the matter on my part. As a matter of fact, I neither solicited nor subsequently received the slightest remuneration from the Sultan or anybody else for a task the arduous and perilous nature of which I was far from realizing at the time, and the outcome of which was a journalistic triumph for the *New York Herald*.

The impression I gained from this interview was that the Sultan was sincere in his wish to get to know the true state of affairs. He believed that the revolutionary activity of the Armenians, connived at by Russia, had been the primary cause of the massacres in Asia Minor as in Constantinople, and that the governors of the different provinces had done their best to protect the innocent and punish the guilty. Abdul Hamid is not the only autocrat who has found it an impossible task to get at the truth, the whole truth, and nothing but the truth. For it goes without saying that His Majesty's estimate of what had taken place was based on partial and incomplete information. On the other hand, our journey furnished us with abundant evidence that the Sultan's views were not without some justification, and that, as a rule, the governors of the different provinces we traversed were men of tried capacity and integrity. Viewed from this distance of time, there can be no doubt that the policy of the Sultan in excluding foreign journalists from Armenia was a mistaken one. It resulted in a one-sided version of the events becoming generally accepted—the lie with twenty-four hours' start, according to Napoleon, is immortal—and it gave opportunities for "writing up" atrocities without any of the extenuating features which provoked them obtaining publicity.

It is not my purpose to render an exact account of our journey, for such would fill a volume. This was done at the time by the late Dr. Hepworth,[4] who did not very long survive the fatigues of the journey, which at his time of life, he being then over sixty years of age, was a most arduous undertaking. My aim will be to give some incidents of our journey, the impressions which have remained in my mind as illustrative of the aspect of the country we passed through as we saw it, and the conversations we had with the people we came in contact with.

> 4. "Through Armenia on Horseback." By the Rev. George H. Hepworth. London and New York, 1898.

The ostensible object of the expedition was to report upon the schools in the different provinces to be traversed, but behind this was obviously the intention of obtaining information outside the usual official channels with regard to the disturbances which had taken place in the year 1895 in that mysterious country which Europeans are in the habit of calling Armenia, although the number of Armenians distributed over an area about as large as France and Germany combined, making every allowance for the unreliability of statistics, can scarcely exceed a million and a half, whereas in the Russian provinces bordering on Asiatic Turkey there are probably even more, of whom, however, the world never hears anything. The route of our journey, as drawn up with the Sultan's approval, would take us through Anatolia, Kurdistan, Mesopotamia, and Syria. We were to proceed by sea to Trebizond, and starting from thence to reach Erzeroum; from there to push on to Van, thence to Bitlis, to Diarbekir, and to Biredschik on the Euphrates; thence to Aintab in Syria, and on to Alexandretta, where we would take ship back to Constantinople. By this route we would traverse four out of the five so-called Armenian vilayets;[5] Erzeroum, Van, Bitlis, and Diarbekir, leaving Mamuret ül Aziz out of our itinerary. This plan was carried out with the exception that we omitted Van owing to the severity of the weather and the uncertainty of being able to keep within the projected time limit. Little did we realize what hardships we were to experience, although we had been warned at Constantinople that such a journey—never an easy one, and usually undertaken in the spring, summer, or autumn—involved very serious risks in the depth of winter, when snowstorms or floods might possibly keep us for weeks together in remote places. The chance of being attacked by Kurdish tribes, of catching some disease owing to the lack of all hygienic conditions in the country, the primitive nature of the accommodation, sleeping on the bare floor side by side with camels, buffaloes, oxen, horses, and dogs all in a state far removed from cleanliness, lastly the unaccustomed food: these were all matters for consideration.

> 5. The term vilayet is derived from the Arabic ejalet, and signifies a governorship—an area—a district such as would be administered by

a pasha; thus a so-called "pasha tik," or staathoudership. Hence the term "Vali" stands for the administrator of a vilayet. The vilayet of Erzeroum, for instance, has an area of nearly 50,000 square kilometres, with 645,000 inhabitants.

On a black windy November morning we started in the Austrian Lloyd steamer *Daphne*, and steamed through the Bosphorus, on our way to the Black Sea, our destination being Trebizond. Our little party was quite representative in its character. His Excellency Sirry Bey, one of the secrétaires traducteurs of the Palace, was in charge of the expedition. Halid Bey, his secretary, a fat, good-natured, harmless young Turk, was always busy taking notes. Two colonels of cavalry, aides-de-camp of the Sultan, were attached to the expedition, and six sergeants of cavalry (Suwarie Tschaoush) formed a military escort in case of unforeseen contingencies. One of these officers, Colonel Tewfik Bey, was an easy-going, lymphatic cavalryman, whose big travelling portmanteau was a horse's entire load by itself, although all the other members of the expedition restricted themselves to small hand-bags in consideration of the difficulties of transport. The other officer, Colonel Rushti Bey, was the most interesting personality of our party, as a specimen of the aristocratic, carefully brought up Turk. A young fair-headed, handsome man, he was indefatigable—the first up and on horseback in the morning and never seeming to tire. He did not smoke or touch any wine or spirits. His bearing was chivalrous, and though not given to expansiveness, he was a man of the kindliest disposition. We had a Doctor Wallisch, a Hungarian in the Turkish service, on board, who was on his way to an appointment in Van. Fortunately for the party we managed to persuade him to accompany us on the whole of our journey. Our interpreter, Hermann Chary, an excitable little Roumanian Jew, who spoke eight or ten languages, was the same man I had picked up in Salonica in the spring of the year.

We encountered very rough weather in the Black Sea, which interfered with our enjoyment of the fine scenery on the shore of Asia with its forest-clad hills, some of them already covered with snow. This journey in the company of staunch Moslems who would spread their little rugs on the deck at sunrise and sunset, and pray silently with their faces turned towards Mecca, was a new sensation to Dr. Hepworth and myself. An awkward incident took place one day during the voyage. The cooking on board as well as the bill of fare was "Frank" (*i.e.* European), and on one occasion roast pork formed an item of the menu. So cunningly was it prepared that none of us was able to detect it except Dr. Hepworth, whose partiality for pork was so strong that his first request on entering a restaurant in Paris, Vienna, or Constantinople was for a pork chop, and when he had made it disappear, for another pork chop. In the ecstasy of a delighted palate he proclaimed aloud that we were partaking of his favourite dish, "roast pork"! Never shall I forget the dismay that spread over the faces of the Turks present when this disclosure was made. In order to save the situation I tried to make out that Dr. Hepworth was mistaken, but finally we all lapsed into silence as the best way out of the difficulty, since the defilement was beyond question.

The weather continued so rough that we were a long time in doubt whether we should be able to stop on our way, as nowhere along the coast was there a sheltered harbour. Only with great difficulty did we disembark for a few hours at Kerasoun and at Samsoun, the seat of large tobacco factories. At Samsoun we reviewed the school-children and saw for the first time a primitive type of plough, and carts with solid wooden wheels drawn by oxen—varying probably little from those in use in the time of Abraham.

Trebizond is picturesquely situated on the shore of the Black Sea at the mouth of the River Moutschka, at the base of a chain of mountains rising gradually to an altitude of 1600 metres, culminating in the thickly wooded Kotal Dagh, 3410 metres high. Even here there is no harbour, and in stress of weather ships have to seek refuge at Platana, two hours and a half distant by steam. The city forms the starting-point of the caravans to Persia; but these have now strong competitors in the Russian railway from Batoum and the caravans from the Persian Gulf. In consequence of these developments the traffic of the interior is declining. Yet Trebizond remains, next to Smyrna, the most important city of Asiatic Turkey, and previous to the Armenian disturbances of the years 1895–96 contained a population of 35,000 inhabitants. At that time, however, a large migration to Russia and Constantinople began, and this was still in progress when we arrived there. More than half of the population consisted of Moslems, with 8000 Greeks and 6000 Armenians, the lower classes being the so-called Lazis, an unruly tribe, from whom the Turks draw their best sailors. Trebizond has an Armenian Archbishop and twenty Christian churches, as well as an American missionary station. All the Turkish mosques were once Christian places of worship.

We were sitting in the dining-room of the Hôtel d'Italie looking out upon the dark waters of the Black Sea rolling menacingly far away to the horizon, when a dark-bearded, slimly built man with a low forehead and ferret-like eyes approached us. He was a Russian Armenian, a doctor of medicine, who had come to Trebizond to set up in practice. He did not care a fig for politics and was silent. He was absorbed in his own profession—that of getting on in the world.

Prominent in his quaint costume and mannerism was a young professor of philology from a university of Northern Europe. He was about twenty-five years of age and believed he knew everything worth knowing in geography, philology, and politics. His sympathies were all with the Christian "brothers."

He had come over from Russia, where, in the pursuit of his philological calling, he had rummaged over the worm-eaten parchments of sundry Christian monasteries, and had caught from these the current term of "brothers"—meaning that the lowliest Christian is a "brother," and the Moslem Turk at best an infidel stranger. He laid down the law without hesitation. "I never condemn a whole people," he exclaimed; "I say that the vices of a people are always the fault of an autocratic Government." Here was a specimen of the learned European, caught young in Turkey, returning home with all the kudos which a few months—or even years—added to a smattering familiarity with Oriental languages, can confer, to be looked upon by his friends as an authority on the Eastern question, and possibly, later on, to champion the claims of the suffering "brothers" in the East in the legislative Chamber of his native land!

The sun had sunk in the west. It was twilight and we were sitting alone, when there entered an American missionary. A few preliminaries revealed the fact that we had to deal with a worthy, excellent man, past middle age—a teacher of the Gospel whose range of interests did not necessarily exclude politics.

"Yes, sir, it is a hard, laborious life, but we keep pegging away," he said in the course of conversation. "No newspapers, railways, or telegraphs: no means of communication with one's friends. It is like living in another world. And what a cesspool it is—fifty feet deep, and, do what we may, we can only disinfect the surface. Formerly, when I first came here, thirty years ago, it was very different. We were encouraged to work, and enjoyed every liberty; also we largely increased the number of our flock; but now," he added despondently, "it is all reaction."

"No wonder," I rejoined, "the past has bred revolution."

"Yes, I admit there has been a revolutionary movement, but not fostered by us. We have always inculcated obedience to the authorities."

"But do I understand you rightly that a well-known revolutionist was one of your pupils?"

"Yes, and I always refused to believe that he had anything to do with the revolutionists."

"Do you refuse to believe so now?"

"No, I am grieved to say."

"Now tell me," I continued, "how are things over in Russia—a Christian country?"

"Far worse than here," he answered in excited tones. "The Russians are much more intolerant—much more reactionary than the Turks. Why, if the

Russians ever come here, they will turn us missionaries neck and crop out of the country."

Thereupon we parted, and I left the hotel in search of a breath of fresh air and came upon an Israelite.

"Why, sir," he began, "those Armenians are an accursed race. To think of the position which they once held in Turkey, after having managed, in the course of generations, to get nearly all the wealth of the country into their hands, and to fill some of the best paid appointments! If they had ventured to play their revolutionary game in Russia, the Russians would not have left a man of them alive. I tell you they are accursed. In our Jewish hooks it is written—written three thousand years ago—that they shall not prosper, that their seed shall be wasted."

Among the men who were credited with a large share in the cruel measures of repression said to have been carried out by different Turkish high officials against the Armenians, the name of Marshal Chakir Pasha, Imperial Commissioner for the introduction of reforms in Anatolia, stood foremost. The story that the Marshal, who was at Erzeroum in the month of October 1895, at the time of the Armenian rising, had, like a human bloodhound, stood, watch in hand, when asked for orders, and decided that the work of knocking the Armenians on the head was to continue for another hour and a half—some versions say two hours—went almost the round of the world. It was told to me in Constantinople by a person of distinction and impartiality, and although this did not amount to proof positive, I could hardly resist the conviction that there must be something in the tale, bearing in mind the exceptional source of my information. I had also heard that more than one of the diplomatic representatives of the Great Powers at Constantinople, notably Sir Philip Currie, had repeatedly but vainly urged the Sultan to recall the Marshal. I was therefore in a somewhat expectant frame of mind when I learnt that the redoubtable pasha was staying in Trebizond with his whole staff. Its principal members consisted of Hassib Effendi, formerly Turkish Consul-General at Tiflis in the Caucasus, and since in like capacity at Teheran; Danish Bey, formerly First Secretary of the Turkish Embassy at St. Petersburg; and Demeter Mavrocordato Effendi.

Marshal Chakir Pasha had had a distinguished career. Educated at the military school of Pancaldi, at Constantinople, he was afterwards attached to the Turkish état-major. Quitting that post after a time, he entered the Administrative Department, and became within a short space of time Governor in succession of Bosnia, Bulgaria, and Bagdad. Subsequently he rejoined the army, and held a command in Montenegro during the war, and later on was present at the memorable Shipka Pass battles. After the Russo-

Turkish war Chakir returned to Constantinople, and was sent as Turkish Ambassador to St. Petersburg, where he remained for twelve years, and where, so the Russian Consul-General at Erzeroum assured me, he saw the Marshal, the doyen of the Diplomatic Corps, leading the polonaise with the Empress Dagmar as a partner.

Since then Chakir Pasha had been civil and military governor of Crete, and previous to his latest appointment he had been nominated member of the High Military Commission of Inspection, which sat under the presidency of the Sultan at the Palace of Yildiz.

I felt somewhat abashed at the thought of asking such a man a series of questions closely affecting his personal honour. But Chakir himself made my task easy by his well-bred urbanity. He was a short, stout, full-bearded, distinguished-looking man of about sixty years of age, with massive features and bright keen eyes, denoting intelligence and capacity for hard work. I called on him at his official residence with Mavrocordato Effendi, and found him in a small, sparsely furnished apartment, sitting at a plain writing-table, the other members of his staff being also present and seated round the table.

After coffee and a few preliminary remarks, I told the Marshal frankly that I had heard the story of the watch, and that I hoped he would kindly excuse my asking him the true facts of the case. He took my question in very good part, and said in reply that he was perfectly cognizant of the tale, but that he had never considered it incumbent upon himself to take official notice of it—any other notice being, of course, in his position, out of the question. However, he could assure me, he added with a smile, that when the story first reached Erzeroum people who knew the facts of the case smiled at the idea. He could only advise me not to take his assurance one way or the other, but, as I was going to Erzeroum, to make my own inquiries.

Encouraged by the Marshal's manner, I then asked him: "I have been told that a large amount of the trouble in Kurdistan was owing to the Kurds having been armed by the Turkish Government, and that it was your Excellency with whom this measure originated."

"As a matter of fact," he replied, "the Kurds have always been more or less armed, and have often used their arms against the Turkish Government, as you are doubtless aware. The idea of arming the Kurds in a homogeneous military fashion, which has led to the formation of the Hamadiè cavalry regiments (about 40,000 to 50,000 strong), belongs to Marshal Zeki Pasha, the Commander of Erzingian. The Sultan approved of the idea, which was intended to furnish a counterpoise to the Russian Cossack regiments, and asked me to work out the plan, which I did at Constantinople, in my capacity of member of the military commission at Yildiz. I even candidly admit that my sympathies are with these regiments—after all, they are my own countrymen." The Marshal repeated this in a quiet tone of almost apologetic modesty, which had something quaintly touching in its simplicity, and set me thinking how very few men in a similar high position in other countries would have condescended to enter thus into details. I could not help feeling drawn towards the old soldier.

Chakir Pasha was not a man of many words, and several of those present now joined in the conversation, which became general. Only once did the Marshal interpose in a quiet but decisive manner. Danish Bey was in the midst of relating some incident, and suddenly stopped short, for some reason or other, whereupon the Marshal said: "Continue, tell him everything—il n'y a rien à cacher."

As I was personally acquainted with many well-known Turkish officers and diplomatists, our conversation had plenty of points of mutual interest. However, in what follows I only give a résumé of what may interest the outside world. Part of what I have to relate was told in the Marshal's presence, he now and then putting in a word or making some verbal correction, whilst some of the details were given me later in the evening at the hotel by the members of his staff and by other persons later at Erzeroum. I give the facts exactly as they were stated to me by individuals who one and all held responsible positions, and who, in our personal intercourse, which lasted several days, made the impression upon me of being honourable, cultivated men of the world. According to my informants, the original troubles at Trebizond had begun two years previously as a consequence of members of the Armenian revolutionary committee firing in broad daylight on Hamid Pasha, the commander of the garrison, and Bahri Pasha, Governor-General of Van, who happened to be at Trebizond at the time, and was walking with Razi Khan, the Persian Consul-General. Both pashas were wounded.

"With regard to the interior, signs of coming trouble were apparent a long time back. In some districts, where the Kurdish chiefs had been accustomed for centuries past to do all their business with the Armenian merchants and bankers in the towns, their mutual relations were of the most cordial character. The Kurds were even in the habit of staying in the houses of their Armenian friends when they came to town. Gradually a change came over the scene. The Kurds met strange faces in the towns, and the manner of the Armenian merchants visibly changed. Russian Armenian journalists from Tiflis became regular visitors, and the assumption is that they influenced the Armenian element in the direction of discontent and revolt. That they were able to do so is the more unaccountable as the Armenian language and the Armenian schools have always been entirely free, and in Turkey the Armenians are exempted from military service—a most distasteful profession to them—on paying a nominal sum. Moreover, the Armenians have been able, in the course of centuries, to gather into their hands the greater part of the wealth of the country. The Armenian 'bakal,' or village grocer, holds a great number of the Turkish peasantry in the perpetual bondage of usury. In Russia, on the other hand, the Armenians are rigorously drafted into the army, and are generally sent to serve their time in districts far away from their homes, while their schools and their language are interfered with by a severe censorship.

"When the insurrectionary movement was ripe, the men who appeared on the scene gave themselves the name of 'Fedaïs,' or the 'Sacrificed for the country.' This is the sobriquet which the notorious Armenian revolutionist, Daniel Tschoueh, applied to himself. Under the pretext of saving his country he roamed through the vilayet of Sivas, where he committed acts of brigandage. And yet this very man was so deficient in physical courage that he died of fear the very day he was brought before the gendarmerie of Sivas. He was originally employed in the mines of Kara Hissar Charki, in the district of the vilayet of Sivas. Among other atrocities which he committed was the murder of the representative of the Procureur-Général of Kara Hissar Charki, as well as his wife and children, on the road to Sivas.

"With regard to the reforms which have since been introduced, it is as well the world should know that the Armenians are only willing to accept such as conform easiest with their idiosyncrasies. But when it is a question of their undertaking obligations which involve certain hardships, such as the post of gendarme, they simply refuse to serve the Imperial Government. It is extremely difficult to find Armenians to serve as gendarmes, and this notwithstanding that the Imperial Government offers them all sorts of inducements. For not only are they well paid, but they are held to be doing military service in acting as gendarmes and are thus freed from the tax for exemption from military service. Instead of serving in the above capacity they prefer posts which offer chances of making money without hard work. Thus they are very eager to be appointed adjunct (muavin) to the kaimakan or to other more or less lucrative official posts."

Chakir Pasha's mission had been to travel all through Kurdistan for the last two years, and the following interesting statements were made sporadically in the further course of my conversations with his suite:

"One of the most remarkable features of this Armenian rebellion was the marvellous rapidity with which news spread among Mussulmans and Armenians alike. Thus, hardly had Sir Philip Currie in the autumn of 1895 telegraphed to Erzeroum to the *locum tenens* of the British Consul that the Sultan had accepted the proposals of the Powers than the gentleman in charge asked for the telegram and interpreted it as portending Armenian autonomy. A newspaper correspondent telegraphed from London to Givon

Schismanian, the Archbishop of Erzeroum, 'Victoire complète' (Armenian: 'Mouzaferiat berke mal'), and the news spread to the farthest limits of Kurdistan. In some places the Kurds decided to make a clean sweep of the Armenians. Chakir Pasha started immediately for Khinis, on the road between Erzeroum and Bitlis, and persuaded the Kurdish beys to remain quiet. Twenty-four hours later it might have been too late." In fact, according to statements of Chakir Pasha's suite, both here and elsewhere he saved many hundred lives by his prompt measures.

The Armenians on their side, so I was assured, fêted the correspondent who had championed their cause in a London newspaper as a national hero, "Le Sauveur de l'Arménie." The Armenians of Erzeroum presented him with a pen set in brilliants; the Armenians of Tiflis gave him whole cases full of presentation plate. The following was subsequently told me by one of Chakir Pasha's staff:

"We were staying at the government house in Van with Chakir Pasha at the end of September '96, when we were unexpectedly informed that the hiding-place of the Armenian insurgents had been discovered. They had entrenched themselves in the gardens of the Armenian quarter of the town, and it would have been extremely difficult to get at them without artillery. Chakir, fearing that the Mussulman population might get beyond control if fighting was at once commenced, told off a large body of troops to cut off the Armenian quarter from the other part of the town. After this was done the Armenian revolutionists were driven out of the town, losing a number of killed and wounded. In the meantime the representative of the Armenian Bishop of Van called upon Chakir Pasha and showed him a telegram which he proposed to send at once to Monsignor Khrimyan, the Armenian *Catholikos* of Etchmiadzin (in Russia), in which he said that, while the Armenians had for six hundred years been contented under the dominion of the Turks, people from abroad were now coming to trouble their tranquillity, and he begged Monsignor Khrimyan to use his influence to prevent such people from coming into the country, as they could only do the Armenians harm. To this Chakir Pasha replied that the telegram in itself was excellent, but it ought to have been sent long ago, and not at the very moment when the insurgents had been discovered by the authorities; that it was a matter of public notoriety that these people had been in Van for two months past, and that the Armenian community had been well aware of the fact, and ought to have apprised the authorities, so that they might distinguish between their friends and their enemies."

Of the members of the suite of Chakir Pasha with whom I had opportunities of talking the most interesting was Mavrocordato Effendi, an Orthodox Catholic, and related to the Greek princely family of the same name. He had previously been Turkish Consul-General at Liverpool and at Barcelona,

Secretary of the Turkish Embassy at Paris, etc., and was a cultured European. He spoke English almost like an Englishman. Community of meals for several days following in stormy, depressing weather brought about mutual confidence and expansion of ideas.

Mavrocordato had not been able to see his young wife and child for fifteen months, as he had accompanied Chakir Pasha in his mission right through Anatolia, or Kurdistan—a country many Europeans will persist in calling "Armenia." He was a hard-working and zealous Turkish official, with the breadth of view of a cultured man of the world.

"Yes," he said in conversation, "the reforms desired by the Powers are now introduced throughout Asiatic Turkey and in full working order. But I do not think much of their practical value. Their spirit is already contained in Turkish law, which is excellently adapted to the needs of this part of the world. Of course we have had abuses: what country, particularly what Eastern country, has not? But we are on the road to improvement. The principal thing we want is a body of honest and capable administrators and minor functionaries, and on your journey through the country you will be able to convince yourself that among Turkish officials in Anatolia the majority, especially among the new appointments, are good men—a great improvement on the old order of things."

"But how about the rumours I hear of appointments depending on the bribery of officials at the Palace in Constantinople?" I asked.

"Do I look like a man who has bribed his way through Palace officials?" he replied. "There may be instances of bribery and peculation, but hardly in connexion with these matters. What Asiatic Turkey is most pressingly in need of are good roads and railways. At the present moment the Mussulman population, which is far worse off than the Christian, is very poor; and the richer the harvest, the poorer they are. For where there is plenty prices decline, as there are no adequate means of transport and no markets. But another difficulty which the Government has to contend with in all its attempts at reform is the conservatism which seems ingrained in everything and everybody Asiatic. It is this that the diplomatists of Europe lose sight of when they, Penelope-like, elaborate one plan of reform after another for the Turkish Empire over a green baize table in some kiosk on the Bosphorus. A little incident will illustrate this. The Sultan sends a capable official to some distant province as kaimakan, or prefect. He has been educated at Constantinople, at the École Civile. He is scrupulously honest, in touch with modern ideas, enthusiastically devoted to his work, and anxious to benefit the people under his care. He endeavours to introduce reforms, beginning with the improvement of the roads of the town where he officially resides. He calls upon the inhabitants to contribute towards this good work. Result:

the Mohammedans and the Armenian population join hands and petition the Government to have the kaimakan removed. He is a modern man: they prefer the old-fashioned do-nothing type of official."

Such was the information my companion and I gathered on the eve of our plunge into the Asiatic domains of the Sultan from some of the men who had been responsible there for the maintenance of order. The time had come for departure. We had spent several days at Trebizond inspecting the bazaar and making some purchases of stores, Dr. Hepworth and myself ordering each a warm sheepskin fur—such as are worn by the peasants and camel-drivers—and after having engaged some tumble-down vehicles and horses, we started on the long journey through the interior of the country to Erzeroum—a matter of eight to ten days' travelling. We took leave of every comfort associated with civilization, such as beds, washing-basins, even tables and chairs, which we only came upon again at the end of our journey at Alexandretta.

CHAPTER V

JOURNEY THROUGH ASIATIC TURKEY: II

My mother Earth!

And thou, fresh breaking Day, and you, ye Mountains,

Why are ye beautiful? I cannot love ye.

And thou, the bright eye of the Universe,

That openest over all, and unto all

Art a delight—thou shin'st not on my heart.

BYRON

ON leaving Trebizond the winding road rises gradually until you reach the tableland of the Taurus, the so-called Armenian Highlands. We took one last look at the Black Sea from a height before it was lost to sight, dark and menacing with its ships lying at anchor.

A feature which struck me with surprise shortly after leaving Trebizond were the Christian monasteries which we passed at intervals, perched high up on the ridge of the hills on either side of us. We were told that they had been tenanted by monks from time immemorial, and that they still inhabit them. Surely here was ocular demonstration in favour of Mohammedan tolerance, since, if the much-spoken-of fanaticism of the Turk had any tangible existence, these monasteries could not possibly have remained unmolested, undefiled, inhabited right through the many centuries during which the country has belonged to the Turks.

Another feature of our journey, which, however, only presented itself to us later on, was equally a matter of surprise to us—imbued as we were with the notion that peaceable Armenians were in daily fear for their lives and property right through the country. We frequently met whole Armenian families, men, women, and children, the women sitting astride their horses, travelling on the road without weapons of any kind.

It was a novel sensation to arrive in the evening at a miserable shed, a barn, a stable, mostly without any windows or other ventilation, termed a "han," in which oxen, buffaloes, and camels were quartered, and to be told that we were expected to pass the night there. But such was destined to be, with few exceptions, our nightly experience for the next few weeks.

On emerging from our stable one morning, long before sunrise, we could scarcely see a yard in front of us. We were surrounded by a thick mist. It rose from an encampment of camels, buffaloes, and horses immediately facing us. It appeared that they had arrived in the evening after us, and, finding the "han" occupied by our party, had camped out all night in the open. The bitter cold had acted in the manner described, causing clouds of steam to rise from the bodies of the animals.

Our first station of any note was a place called Gumysch Hanè, a name which denoted that silver mines were or had been worked in the neighbourhood. Here we changed our carriages for saddle-horses, with which next morning we crossed the Zigana Pass—6000 feet high and one of the most perilous sections of our journey now that in the winter, owing to the snow, the road, at its best little better than a bridle-path, was narrowed to the breadth of a mere wooden plank, with yawning ravines on the off-side of us. It was here that we met the most thrilling experiences of our whole journey—namely, the encountering of caravans of mules, camels, and droves of sheep proceeding in the opposite direction. We were told that only a short time previously on this road a number of camels connected together by ropes had lost their footing and been precipitated into the abyss below. Here I cannot resist the temptation of quoting a passage describing Professor Vambéry's experience over the same road, as it exactly tallies with my own: "On our way we met a long line of over-loaded mules descending amidst the wild screams of their Persian drivers. It is a rare sight to watch them advancing with the utmost care, without any accident upon the slippery path cut into the rock, scarcely two spans wide, flanked by the bottomless abyss. And yet it is a very unusual thing for a mule to be precipitated into the abyss yawning along the path. If ever it happens it is in winter. The danger is greatest when two caravans happen to meet face to face. In order to avoid such an encounter big bells, heard at a great distance, are used by them, warning the caravans to keep out of each other's way. The continuously steep ascent lasted over four hours. There is hardly a worse road in all Asia, yet this is the only commercial road which connects Armenia with Persia, nay, Central Asia with the West. During the summer hundreds of thousands of these animals are traversing this route, going and coming, loaded with the products of Asia and the manufactures of Europe."[6]

    [6]. "Arminius Vambéry: Life and Adventures." London, 1890: pp. 38–39.

Thus our feeling of relief was great when we had happily crossed the Zigana Pass without further trouble than the anxious moments involved in dodging the camels, mules, and sheep we met; their tinkling bells warning us of their approach, whilst we in our turn warned them with our own bells hanging at our horses' necks. There was only one critical moment, at least for me, when my horse became restive, for it looked as if intent on negotiating the abyss. I rose in my stirrup, ready to jump off on the inside, so as to allow of my mount taking the fatal leap alone.

On the evening of November 21 we arrived at Baiburt, the largest town in the Armenian Highlands after Erzeroum, from which it is still 105 kilometres away. Baiburt is about 1638 metres above sea-level, and occupies an important commercial and strategic position. It is situated on the fringe of the Armenian Highlands and the Pontine mountain range, and forms a connecting link between the two. Previous to the Russo-Turkish war of 1877 it possessed 10,000 inhabitants, which have since diminished to about one-half. It had also been taken by the Russians under General Paskiewitsch in 1828, and had suffered severely. An observant German traveller,[7] visiting the place nearly seventy years ago, before the present German fashion of treating everything Turkish as *couleur de rose*, described Baiburt as giving one a foretaste of "those desolate, decayed, half-ruined, and nearly deserted towns which, from here right throughout the whole of Asiatic Turkey up to the Persian frontier, form a sequence of progressive misery." These words require little variation to describe the appearance of the place when we came there. For instance, we were assured that there was not a single qualified doctor in the town. And yet, although a poverty-stricken place, it was still possible to meet with people bearing expensive weapons on their person, for, like the nomads of old, the Asiatic Turk usually carries all his portable property about with him. At least, so much might be inferred from the fact that I bought a beautiful damascene dagger with a solid silver sheath and handle from a servant for six Turkish pounds.

    7. Reisen von Moritz Wagner. Leipzig, 1852.

We started early next morning, having exchanged saddle-horses for sledges, and arrived at sunset at our destination, another wretched "han" at the foot of the renowned Kop Dagh, which we were to cross in the morning, the pass being 8000 feet above sea-level. The summit is variously given as between 10,000 and 11,000 feet above sea-level. Owing to the danger of being delayed by snow-drifts, relays of workmen were engaged during the night to clear a path for our sleighs through the snow. It was arranged that we should start before daybreak, between four and five in the morning. The journey turned out to be a somewhat exciting affair. We started by the dim light of lanterns, first crossing a frozen stream. Our horses, at times up to their bodies in snow, had the greatest difficulty; at others our sleighs were repeatedly on the point of turning over and landing us in the unknown. Luckily, we were not troubled with the boisterous wind we had feared we might encounter at the summit; and after several hours of laborious ascent we crossed the pass in all safety, if not in comfort, owing to the bitter cold of that region. In the course of the day we met a solitary horseman on his way to the pass. He was a Canadian missionary, with whom we exchanged greetings.

Travellers unite in describing the scenery in this part of the Armenian Highlands as of surpassing beauty. In the winter we saw nothing of the wonderful effects of atmosphere and colour which form such a striking feature of the country, as the whole landscape up to the horizon was one mass of snow-covered mountains, somewhat resembling in character and outline the broad convex cupolas of a Turkish mosque, say the Aja Sophia of Constantinople.

As the sun breaks in the early morning on the Kop Dagh, a vision presents itself to the eye as of the bursting forth of the light of heaven. It reminded me of some of the most ambitious efforts of Gustave Doré in his illustrations of the Bible.

Look, how the floor of heaven

Is thick inlaid with patines of bright gold;

There's not the smallest orb which thou behold'st,

But in his motion like an angel sings,

Still quiring to the young-eyed cherubims:

Such harmony is in immortal souls;

But, whilst this muddy vesture of decay

Doth grossly close it in, we cannot hear it.

Merchant of Venice, v.

Arrived at the summit of the pass, the endless panorama of a snow-covered, undulating tableland at our feet is as that of a mythical world, majestic, almost terrible in the total absence of all human habitations as far as the eye could reach towards the horizon—weird in its vast expanse, all covered with snow.

We reached Erzeroum in the afternoon of November 24. The grim-looking old fortress was dimly perceptible from afar through the dry wintry mist, dominated by a background of hills rising considerably higher than the plateau upon which it is situated. As we drew near, our cavalcade careered along *ventre à terre*, the horses of our cavalry escort foaming and bleeding at the mouth as their riders urged them on at a furious pace in order to enable us to reach our destination before dark—the only instance in all our journey when I saw horses at all hardly used. Here, as later at Bitlis and Diarbekir, our arrival had been expected: the roofs of the houses were crowded with inhabitants—women and children among them—eager to obtain a sight of the remarkable visitors as our cortège drove past and proceeded through the narrow streets to our quarters at one of the public offices or konaks in the town. Our camp-beds were promptly fixed up and we could look for a few days' rest after the exertions of our journey. Here we found ourselves in the interior of Asia.

Professor Vambéry, visiting Erzeroum more than fifty years ago, gives a depressing description of the place. The houses were already built in Eastern fashion, the walls of stone and mud running irregularly in zigzag line, with windows looking out in the yard rather than the street, secret entrances, and other little things characteristic of Eastern houses.[8] "Evidences of the poverty of the inhabitants of Erzeroum meet the eye in whatever direction one may look. The dirt, the squalor, and the underground dwellings are unbearable. The smell of their food, which they cook by the fire made of a fuel called tezek (cattle dung), is especially loathsome." This description tallies with our own experience. The hardships we had undergone—notably the unpalatable food spread out before us on the ground—quickened our longing to arrive at Erzeroum, which, to our imagination, tired by the contrast we expected it to offer to the places we had passed through, already presented itself in glowing colours. Dr. Hepworth and I had ceased to enjoy a meal long before we reached Erzeroum, and had it not been that M. Maximow, the Russian Consul, generously lent us his Armenian cook, who accompanied us during the remainder of our journey, we both might well have succumbed to its hardships.

    [8]. "Life and Adventures of Arminius Vambéry." London, 1890: p. 41.

Erzeroum is the capital of the vilayet of that name, and is situated on a plateau thirty-eight kilometres long by twenty-two broad, stretched out at an altitude of 6000 feet above sea-level. It is dominated by mountains of even greater altitude, near to which the Kara Sua, or Western Euphrates, has its source not far from the city. The town is a very old settlement. The word "Erzeroum" is a corruption of "Arzen-er-rum," *i.e.* the town of Arzen of the Romans—in contradistinction to a neighbouring town of the same name which was a Syro-Armenian settlement in antiquity. In the beginning of the fifth century of our era Erzeroum was converted into a fortress by Anatolius, one of the generals of Theodosius the Younger, in honour of whom it was christened Theodosiopolis, a name it retained until the middle of the eleventh century. In more recent times it has been repeatedly occupied by the Russians, as in 1829 and 1878. To-day Erzeroum has 39,000 inhabitants, half of which are made up of Armenians, Persians, and a few Greeks. Persia, Russia, England, and the United States are represented by Consuls. It also contains a missionary station. Erzeroum is approached by a modern but rudely constructed chaussée.

We had looked forward to visiting the bazaar, in the hope of being able to get hold of some bargains in rare coins, old Turkish swords or daggers; but we were doomed to disappointment here, as also later on at Bitlis and Diarbekir. Whatever may have been the chances of bargains in times gone by, there was nothing left worth picking up when we were there. Of greater interest than the bazaar was the street in which the sword-makers plied their trade beside each other as in their guilds in the Middle Ages. They worked according to primitive methods, with rude tools and weighing scales, but apparently under dignified independent conditions, and seemed to take a pride in their art, which allowed of a workman putting his best efforts into his work and claiming a price in accordance therewith. They showed us some beautiful specimens of damascene blades and gold-inlay work, which induced us to have our names inscribed in Turkish characters by the same process on the barrels of our Winchester rifles. But even their trade, we were told, is not what it used to be. Many of their best workmen (Armenians) had emigrated to Russia, though some had since returned. Altogether the influence of Russia loomed large over the place. The driver of our sleigh, an elderly man, had been a prisoner in Russia. We were told there was a great scarcity of wood in the district, but though there are plenty of forests over the borders in Russia, the Russian authorities would not allow the timber to be exported to Turkey, as they pursued a policy of "drying up" all Turkish means of communication.

We next passed through a street almost monopolized by black amber workers. They drew their raw material from Persia, beyond Lake Van, but here again the workmen told us sadly that they had to procure their tools from Russia. Altogether, I gained the impression that the "Double Eagle" would not have much trouble in ousting the "Crescent" from these parts; though the more intelligent of the community, and, significant to note, Armenians among them, did not view the prospect with favour. The maligned Turk, if hopelessly backward from a practical point of view, is yet in many ways more pliable and conciliatory than the Russian. The market-place, with its endless array of carts and booths, was largely peopled by Persians, who do most of the carrying trade, the retailing business being here, as elsewhere, in the hands of the Armenians. Of Jews there was hardly any trace. We were told that they could not compete with the Armenians.

It would be difficult for people living under European conditions to realize the prestige which our party enjoyed in these distant parts. For the moment we figured as direct ambassadors from the Sultan and the public opinion of the outer world, thus eclipsing the status of the Governor-General himself. And yet in some respects there was a natural homeliness about our intercourse which is usually foreign to the Western world. Thus, when we had finished our dinner, at which we were waited upon by a host of servants—our six cavalry sergeants among others—and rose from our seats, those who had waited upon us sat down quite naturally in the places we had just vacated and proceeded to take their own dinner from the rich supply of viands left on the table as almost a matter of course. Nor did this unusual familiarity detract in the least from the extreme deference and goodwill with which we were waited upon by everybody deputed to our service.

With the object of our journey in view we called successively upon Mr. Graves, the British Consul; Mohamed Cherif Reouf Pasha, the Governor-General (Vali); M. Roqueferrier, the French Consul; and M. V. Maximov, the Russian Consul-General. To each of these gentlemen we put the question whether he believed in the truth of the tale about Chakir Pasha and the watch-in-hand episode. M. Roqueferrier ridiculed the story. "Ce sont des histoires inventées à plaisir," he said, and added a few words of high personal appreciation of Chakir Pasha.

The Russian Consul, M. Maximov, said: "It is not my business to deny the truth of such tales. All I can tell you is, 'que Chakir Pasha est un brave homme—un homme de très bon cœur.' I have known him for years, he is a friend of mine." Mr. Graves, the British Consul, said: "I was not here at the time, nor have I spoken to Chakir Pasha about the matter, but the Vali assured me that it was not true, and that is quite sufficient for me, as I should believe implicitly any personal statement of Reouf Pasha."

"Do you believe that any massacres would have taken place if no Armenian revolutionaries had come into the country and incited the Armenian population to rebellion?" I asked Mr. Graves.

"Certainly not," he replied. "I do not believe that a single Armenian would have been killed."

Mr. Graves is a weighty authority, and if he is in Turkey to-day I feel sure he will not object to my citing him in this important matter.

Let it suffice, we did not meet a single person in Erzeroum, whatever his nationality, race, or creed might have been, who attached the slightest credence to a story which, cunningly invented and circulated broadcast, not only cruelly slandered a man of integrity, but did a deal of harm to his country in the public opinion of the world.

The position of Vali or Governor-General of a Turkish province has come to be associated with an unenviable notoriety in the estimation of a large section of the European public. Not unnaturally, a great share of the responsibility for the wild vengeance of the mob rests with those invested with supreme authority, and where the person wielding this authority has been unequal to its grave responsibilities rumour has stepped in and has credited Turkish officials in general with every imaginable crime.

There are doubtless bad Valis as there are bad men in other stations of life, and we were on the look-out for one in order to make an example of him. Alas that I can only give my experience of a good Vali, Mohamed Cherif Reouf Pasha, Governor-General of the first-class vilayet of Erzeroum.

When General Grant visited Jerusalem, he found Reouf Pasha in the position of Governor of that wonderful city. A strong friendship sprang up between the thin-lipped, taciturn general and the suave, courtly, and yet most simple-mannered pasha. Their meeting had taken place many years previously, but Reouf still loved to talk of Grant, whom he recognized as one of the few truly great men he had come across in his lifetime. And as for Grant's opinion of Reouf, I understand from a reliable source that, before leaving Jerusalem, Grant assured him that if he were again elected President of the United States, he would ask the Sultan to send him as Turkish Minister to Washington.

Reouf Pasha belongs to one of the oldest Turkish families. His father, Osman Pasha, was Governor-General of Bosnia during the last ten years of his life. Reouf Pasha was educated at home, under the care of special tutors, and later on his father sent him to Paris to complete his studies. Among the successive appointments of a long and honourable career may be mentioned those of kaimakan and moutesarrif in Roumelia, Bosnia, and Syria, and twelve years' governorship of Jerusalem—one of the most difficult posts in the Empire. From thence Reouf Pasha was sent to Beirut as Governor-General, then in succession to Damascus, Bitlis, and Kharput, displaying everywhere the qualities of justice and mercy. His activity was ceaseless, and order followed his advent everywhere. He was appointed to his present very responsible and onerous position just one week prior to the breaking out of the Armenian rebellion in October 1895.

In the following words I endeavour to sum up the information I gained from various sources, notably the Consular representatives in Erzeroum, concerning Reouf Pasha's work as Vali of that province.

"Those who have carefully watched the Governor-General in his endeavours to stay the misfortunes of those black hours, to limit their area and repair the damage done, cannot resist the impression that no trouble whatever would have taken place if he had had time to guard against it.

"When Reouf Pasha was appointed to Erzeroum it was already too late. He did what could be done to stop the impending evil, sending the soldiers and gendarmes to the most threatened spots, arresting pillaging Kurds and having them summarily shot, notably those who had come from the vilayet of Bitlis and had advanced as far as Kighi. Reouf Pasha caused between eighty and ninety Mohammedan Turks to be shot during those critical days.

"As soon as the murderous crisis had subsided Reouf Pasha did all in his power to make amends for the damage done. He caused searching investigations to be made all over Erzeroum, and wherever stolen property was found it was restored to its rightful owners. A large portion of what had been pillaged was taken away from the pillagers and delivered back. He also organized a public subscription, the amount of which enabled over four hundred mechanics to resume their occupation.

"Once tranquillity was restored, Reouf Pasha reorganized the gendarmerie and the police so effectually that whilst they were kept more strictly in hand than ever before, they were most successful in arresting a number of Armenian agents-provocateurs and revolutionary emissaries, such notably as Aram Aramian and Armenak Dermonprejan. In the affair of Alidjekrek, in 1896, a number of Armenian revolutionists came over the Russian frontier towards Alaskird. Reouf Pasha, informed in time, sent a body of gendarmcs to meet them, with the result that three were killed and the remainder took flight back to Russia.

"A number of secret stores of arms in different places—Passen, Sitaouk, etc.—were discovered by the vigilance of Reouf's police, and were safely stowed away. I myself saw some of the muskets seized—they bore a Russian inscription.

"All these results are most satisfactory, and have been obtained quietly, without exciting the feelings of the Mohammedan population. Since Reouf Pasha has been here it can be said that justice is handled in the most satisfactory manner. Several of the Courts of Justice which were in need of a broom have been swept, and now work perfectly. A number of corrupt officials have been made an example of—notably the former commissary of police. In a word, all classes of the population unite in recognizing the beneficent activity of the present Vali of Erzeroum, respecting whose government an English Blue Book contains the following: 'The Vilayet of Erzeroum may be given as a model of administration among the governorships of Asiatic Turkey.'"

The following instance was told me of an Armenian being chosen for preferment by the Vali. He was the second commissary of police at Erzeroum, and had proved himself to be so efficient an officer all through the political troubles that Reouf procured for him the commandership of the order of Medjediè, and also a brevet rank equal to that of major in the Army.

Thus far the information given to me, the main correctness of which I feel I can vouch for.

I was privileged to meet his Excellency on several occasions during our stay in Erzeroum, and nothing could exceed his unvaried courtesy and affability.

Even more than this, he showed a positive anxiety that I should accept no statement from him uncorroborated by independent testimony. Through his kindness every channel of information, whether Armenian, Greek, Hebrew, or Turk, was unreservedly set at my disposal. His pet phrase was: "Si c'est la vérité, dites-le!"

In my personal intercourse with Reouf Pasha I was struck by the extraordinary contrast between his quiet, even gentle manners and the great energy he was credited with. There was little mutual esteem between him and Chakir Pasha. To the mind of the mild, gentle-voiced administrator, the hardy soldier who had been credited with all sorts of dreadful energy was not energetic enough. The characteristic feature of Reouf Pasha's energy seems to have been that it enabled him to conciliate—to turn an enemy into a friend.

Before leaving Erzeroum, we paid a visit to the Armenian school, which is organized on the German plan and includes a commercial and classical curriculum. It had at that time one hundred and thirty-four pupils. It was a bitterly cold day, the playground had been flooded and was a sheet of ice, and a number of boys and grown-ups were skating. One of the masters told me that the whole "American Colony" of Erzeroum came to skate there. I asked "What Americans?" and discovered that there was absolutely only one *bonâ-fide* American in the whole city at that particular moment, and he was Mr. Leo Bergholz, the American Consul, and even he was not a Christian, being of the Jewish persuasion; moreover, he had not yet received his official exequatur. The so-called American Colony consisted entirely of Armenians who had acquired American citizenship and flaunted their cheaply gained nationality in the face of the Turkish authorities.

Later on, at Alexandretta, when our dragoman became ill, an "American" doctor was called in to attend him, and turned out to be a dark Syrian Armenian—a thoroughbred Asiatic. These facts in themselves were not necessarily of a mischievous kind; but nobody who has travelled in those parts can be ignorant of the capital made by these strange Americans out of their exotic nationality, and the trouble they occasionally give to the Turkish authorities by their pretensions, quite independent of the fact that many of these so-called "Americans" were in touch, as they doubtless were in full sympathy, with the Armenian revolutionary movement.

We were heartily glad to leave Erzeroum, for among other inconveniences we found the air so rarefied that the slightest exertion would increase the heart's action and produce a sense of fatigue.

CHAPTER VI

JOURNEY THROUGH ASIATIC TURKEY: III

Rough quarries, rocks and hills whose heads touch heaven,

It was my hint to speak—such was the process;

And of the cannibals that each other eat,

The Anthropophagi, and men whose heads

Do grow beneath their shoulders.

SHAKESPEARE, Othello

WE left Erzeroum on the road to Bitlis in sleighs, roughly constructed from unplaned trunks of trees, which we exchanged for saddle-horses at the first station we stopped at.

Shortly after leaving Erzeroum all vestige of roads whatsoever vanished from our ken, and when we came up with a river—for instance, the Tigris, here called the Murad Su or Black Water—it was always a case of being obliged to ford across, for whatever bridges we saw were in ruins. Neither tree, shrub, nor verdure of any kind met the eye—a perfect wilderness, a country in which, as the Germans say, "the foxes bid good-night to each other, as there is nothing to be got for any of them."

Our Armenian cook Migirditch proved a treasure, more indispensable to us, as it turned out, than our doctor, whose services, fortunately, neither Dr. Hepworth nor I called into requisition during the whole of our journey. This man would gallop alone ahead and reach our evening's destination long before us; for our usual rate of progress could scarcely have exceeded three to four miles an hour. Thus we had not to wait when we arrived, but found a well-prepared meal ready for us. How he managed to find his way when there were no visible roads remains a mystery to me to this day. Altogether, the efficiency, the general readiness of this man, the only one of our party who had a notion how to prepare food in European fashion, furnished an excellent illustration of the adaptability of the Armenians. It helped to explain and justify their ambition to rise in the world out of their easy-going surroundings. Indeed, it is only fair to state that throughout our whole journey the Armenians were the only section of the population which seemed to be at all imbued with Carlyle's gospel of work; which tends to explain their unpopularity with the Turks on economic grounds.

We were not destined to see much of the fauna of the country, which is said to consist of panthers, wolves, hyænas, and many species of the feathered tribe, including buzzard and blackcock. Birds of prey we saw in plenty, hovering in the air above us, chiefly vultures, the presence of which was easily to be explained by the occasional carcasses of dead horses and camels we passed on our way. One day a soldier of our escort shot an eagle. It was only winged when it fell, and thus maimed, the soldier brought it into the shed in which we were lying, where it fluttered about, beating its wings. It was not a pleasant sight to see the noble bird, the emblem of imperial power, being beaten to death in our presence.

On our way we had a striking opportunity of witnessing the pride and attachment the Turks feel towards their family, however humble it may be. Some days after leaving Erzeroum we noticed an old man in peasant costume riding along with us over hill and dale through the snow. He wore pointed slippers and looked like some fierce Saracen chief of old. When we halted for the night, Sirry Bey asked us if we would come over into his shed. He wished us to make the acquaintance of his uncle, who was the old peasant referred to, and who had ridden quite alone from his homestead, many miles away, to meet our party. It was a touching sight to see the pride with which Sirry Bey introduced us to his kinsman. He himself boasted the title of Excellency, and was one of the secretaries of the Sultan, coming direct from the Palace in Constantinople, with all the prestige which this fact carries in the eyes of the inhabitants of the provinces, to whom "Cospoli" (Constantinople) and the Sultan are only second in importance to Mecca and the Kaaba; and yet he took a back seat in the presence of the old peasant, his uncle, and thus his senior in the family. It did one's heart good to see the pleasure with which he introduced us to the old man. We were told by our doctor that when Sirry Bey first met his uncle on the road he embraced him and kissed his hands in token of deference to his age, and to the higher standing in the family given him as uncle in comparison with the nephew.

Our journey through Anatolia also brought us an unforgettable instance of the unselfish fidelity of a Turkish police officer. On starting from Erzeroum he was deputed by the Vali to look after us day and night, to devote himself especially to the care of Dr. Hepworth and myself during our journey from Erzeroum towards Bitlis, as a sacred trust. And faithfully indeed did he carry out his mission. He never let us out of his sight: he brought us in the early morning the water heated over the charcoal fire of the mangal to make our cocoa, helped us on to the horses' backs on starting, forded the river in front of us to make sure we should have a safe crossing, rode by our side until we arrived at our destination, and often lay down beside us at night. One evening we were told that he was due to return to Erzeroum next morning. We called him into the shed in which Dr. Hepworth and myself were to pass the night. In addition to handing him a letter for Reouf Pasha thanking him for the excellent service his officer had rendered us, we offered him a little purse filled with Turkish gold. It was a poignant spectacle to see this poor fellow, whose miserable pay was probably months in arrear, positively refuse to accept anything from us but the letter in which we had borne testimony to his fidelity. There was mental distress in his manner and in the tone of his voice: he, who had probably never in his life handled as much gold as that we offered him, pleading that he could not accept it. "No, no," he cried out; "you have given me the letter saying you are satisfied that I have done my duty." Though Dr. Hepworth was case-hardened by thirty years of American journalism, I saw tears glisten in his eyes.

One day a Turkish colonel rode over from Bayazid, the furthest eastern Turkish frontier station, situated at the foot of the Ala Dagh (10,000 feet high), where he was in command, to bid us welcome to those distant parts. No small feat of horsemanship was this journey for him—over a pathless mountain range through the snow, into which his horse sank at times up to the belly. He was a splendid example of the strong, pure-bred Turanian Turk, equal to any amount of fatigue and exposure. For though we were in the midst of winter, and the distance he had come could have been scarcely less than a two days' ride on horseback, he wore no mantle over his uniform, which barely covered his chest from the piercing blast. He was, besides, what would justly be termed a "jolly good fellow." His saddle trappings, pistol holsters, dagger, and belt were of silver, beautifully inlaid with black and gold—the finest specimens of so-called Circassian, but in reality Armenian, workmanship that I had ever seen, even in the bazaar of Constantinople. Responding to our expressions of admiration, he pressed us to accept the belt and dagger as souvenirs. This we declined to do, as we did not see how we could make him any return. But so determined was he in his generous intentions that he left the articles on my camp-bed, where I found them in the evening. But even then I felt I could not accept such a princely gift from a stranger, and next morning, with Sirry Bey's assistance, I prevailed upon him to take them back.

It was on this section of our journey that we passed through several Circassian villages. The Circassians are a most interesting race, inasmuch as it has hitherto been impossible to discover their relationship to any other Asiatic race; their origin is also unknown beyond the fact that they inhabited the shores of the Black Sea and the Sea of Azov before the Christian era. Their country was ceded to Russia in 1829 by the Peace of Adrianople, but the repressive measures they were subjected to in wars in the Caucasus led to 300,000 out of a total of 400,000 seeking refuge in Turkey, where they have since lived in separate communities, some of which we passed through. They are reputed to be physically the finest race of men and women in these parts, probably in all Asia. From them are drawn many of the stalwart guards to be seen in the Imperial palaces at Constantinople and St. Petersburg, as well as some of the finest women in the harems of the Sultan and the wealthy pashas. The men we saw certainly bore out their reputation for fine physique. Many of them were well over six feet in height, with remarkably fine features, well-shaped hands, and the smallest feet I have ever seen with such stature. They were dressed in the well-known Circassian costume, with rows of cartridges on either breast and long daggers peeping out of their girdles. They received us with stately hospitality, but are in general credited with being crafty and treacherous.

What with the desolate nature of the country, hardly a soul being met on the road in a whole day's journey, and the wretched character of our nightly accommodation, this section of our journey included our roughest experiences. The wildness of the conditions was brought home to us in an unpleasant manner by the fierceness of the huge dogs in the villages. They had to be kept at bay with drawn swords by our escort.

We were now well into the mountain fastnesses of Kurdistan—a fact revealed to us by the ever-increasing escort of Kurdish horsemen that joined our cavalcade: a motley gathering of fierce-looking men armed to the teeth, dressed in their national costume, the head covered with a black hood which gave them a peculiarly demoniac appearance. They bade us a kindly welcome to their villages and underground dwellings.

Before we left Constantinople, my friend Ahmed Midhat Effendi had given me a letter written in Turkish characters which he said would ensure us a kindly welcome in every part of the Sultan's dominions. So indeed it turned out to be on different occasions, notably one evening when we halted in a Kurdish village and passed the night in the underground dwelling of a chieftain. We squatted down on the floor in a circle, when Colonel Rushti Bey brought out Midhat Effendi's letter, the careful calligraphy of which called forth the admiration of those present, and read its contents out aloud. Therein was set forth how the proprietor of one of the greatest journals in the world, moved by a noble impulse to see that justice was done to the Osmanli, had sent "two fearless, impartial, and, above all, learned men of letters to see things as they were with their own eyes, and to report thereon to the outer world." It was quite an impressive spectacle to see these men of supposed lawless proclivities listening devoutly to the description of our mission therein set forth, to champion the truth against the slander of the "Frank," ignorant of the justice of the Turkish cause. As each sentence was read out in a clear, sympathetic voice, the interest of the audience grew visibly, until at the close, as with one voice, those present ejaculated in unison, "May Allah bless and protect them!" It was an impressive scene in its simplicity and evident sincerity.

Early the next morning, when we departed, our hosts declined to take any payment for their hospitality; on the other hand, they pressed us to accept presents from them—daggers and belts richly inlaid with silver and gold ornamentation, even a horse each to Dr. Hepworth and myself. All these we declined, but I could not refuse the skin of a bear which the chief himself had killed with his dagger in a regular "hand to paw" encounter, as we were assured. It served as a rug in my study for years afterwards. Even when we left, the kindliness of our hosts was not exhausted, for a number of Kurds accompanied us for a long distance on horseback—an attention which was extended to us right through that part of the country wherever we stopped. This escort grew sometimes to such dimensions that on occasions we were accompanied by several hundred horsemen, most of whom belonged to the irregular force of cavalry known by the name of Hamidiè, already referred to. They rode ahead of us, galloped in circles round us, shouting lustily and firing off their rifles and otherwise demonstrating the festive frame of mind into which the visit of the Padishah's representatives among his unruly vassals had plunged them. The further we penetrated into the country the more numerous became the native escort which joined and followed us from station to station amid lively demonstrations of good feeling.

One morning, on emerging from the underground mud hut in which we had passed the night as guests of a Kurdish chief, we caught a glimpse of Mount Ararat, towering 17,000 feet out of the clouds in front of us. According to our map this marked the most easterly point of our itinerary, and Mount Ararat can scarcely have been less than forty miles away from us. Our own elevation must have been about 6000 to 7000 feet above the level of the sea; this circumstance, together with the clearness of the atmosphere, enabled us to make out the outline of the giant mountain quite distinctly a long way down to its base. For, unlike all the other mountains we saw on our journey, Mount Ararat stands by itself, rising in the form of a single cone from the plain.

In the further course of our journey, not far from Bitlis we caught a glimpse of Lake Van to our left. Indeed, we almost skirted its shores, though it lay beneath us covered with ice and snow. The lake is situated about 5000 feet above sea-level: thus our own altitude must have been considerably more.

Bitlis is on the caravan road from Erzeroum to Mosul, about ten miles to the south-west of Lake Van on about the same level, namely, 5000 feet, on the banks of the Tigris, with about 39,000 inhabitants. We stayed at the konak of the Governor in the centre of the town, on an elevation which was formerly a fortress, at the foot of which the usual Oriental bazaar stretches through several narrow streets. Bitlis has belonged to the Turks since 1514, when it was occupied by Sultan Selim I. Here we were once more in touch with civilization by means of the post office and a telegraph station, and spent a few days interviewing different people—an English Vice-Consul, some missionaries and Armenians—and choosing horses for the continuation of our journey on horseback to Diarbekir, which took several days and passed without incident.

Diarbekir lies on the Tigris, which is spanned by an old stone bridge, across which we rode, the river itself being navigable only for rafts. Situated nearly 2000 feet above sea-level, the ancient fortress of Diarbekir has an interesting history. At one time a Roman colony, it became the see of a Christian bishop in A.D. 325. Enlarged by the Emperor Constantine in the fourth century, it was conquered and devastated by Timur in 1373 and fell under Turkish sway in the year 1513, when, like Bitlis, it was taken by Sultan Selim I. To-day Diarbekir is much diminished in size and importance, but still possesses about 34,000 inhabitants, twenty mosques, an Armenian school, and a bazaar, in which, however, there was nothing of interest to be seen. There were only three European residents when we came to Diarbekir: an old Franciscan monk, a French Vice-Consul, and an English Consul, Mr. Alexander Waugh, now British Consul in Constantinople. This gentleman bade us a warm welcome, and his hospitality, notably the meals we partook of at his house, one of which was our Christmas dinner, formed the one bright recollection in the dreary record of our stay. The versions given us by Turks and Armenians of what had occurred in connexion with the Armenian disturbances differed little from those we had already heard elsewhere: that the troubles were brought about in the first instance by revolutionary activity, that the authorities had lost their heads, and that finally the population had got out of hand and had joined in an indiscriminate massacre of Armenians, innocent and guilty.

Our further journey from Diarbekir was also devoid of any incident, and on the evening of December 31 we rode into the picturesque old town of Biredschik, and were quartered in a fairly comfortable konak.

Biredschik is situated about 600 feet above sea-level, on the left bank of the Euphrates, which is navigable here for boats of considerable size. It is surrounded by a fairly preserved wall, protected by a castle built on rocks. Biredschik is the most renowned of the places, known to both the Romans and the Seleucides, which were used for crossing the Euphrates, a purpose for which Biredschik has been much in use down to the present day. It numbers several thousand Armenians among its inhabitants. Here we saw the New Year in, and started next morning for Aintab, crossing the Euphrates, which is here very broad, with our saddle-horses, in large shallow-bottomed pontoon-boats. The country offered a marked contrast to that which we had hitherto traversed. For whereas we had not seen a tree for weeks together, or a road of any kind for an even longer period, here we suddenly found ourselves among groves of olive-trees and fig-trees, besides other indications of a Southern clime—an agreeable change from the treeless wilderness we had passed through ever since we left Erzeroum.

Not far from Biredschik we rode past Nisib, a village noteworthy through the battle of that name (June 24, 1839), in which the Turks under Hafis Pasha were signally defeated by the Egyptians under Ibrahim Pasha. The renowned Moltke, then a plain Prussian captain, was a looker-on with the Turks on this occasion, and it is said that they owed their defeat to having neglected his advice in the disposition of the troops in that battle.

Our road now took us through a flat country, and our spirits rose under the improved conditions. At mid-day we used to make a halt, tie up the horses, light a fire, and take an improvised lunch in the open. One day we rested beside a stream on the opposite bank of which one of the soldiers had placed a winebottle as a target. The Sultan had presented us each with a revolver on starting, and our Turkish escort were firing away with them at random, without, however, "driving the centre." Dr. Hepworth and I stood aside, looking on somewhat amused, which made the situation rather awkward when Sirry Bey suggested we should join in and have a shot. This, however, we hesitated to do, for the good reason that we had previously tested our revolvers on board ship and found that we could not hit a haystack with them. Finally, Dr. Hepworth also urged me to try my luck; so, not wishing to appear churlish, I took a haphazard aim, and, to my intense surprise, down came the bottle. The others were much impressed, and begged me to repeat the exploit. This, however, I firmly declined to do, preferring to leave them under the impression of my dexterity. Few things struck me more forcibly on that journey than the lack of practice with firearms right through this supposed warlike population. We never came across a single rifle-range on the whole of our journey, and on one occasion when we attended an improvised shooting competition among the Kurds their marksmanship was of a very inferior order, and the behaviour of the competitors so excited that I gained the impression they might resent anybody excelling them at their sport.

We had met few horsemen since we left the land of the Kurds; but after Biredschik they again appeared on the scene. Now, however, they were Syrians, men in white flowing garments—bournous—resembling the Arab costumes familiar through Schreyer's pictures of Algerian life, wielding spears of twelve to fifteen feet in length. They gave us an equally warm reception, and, like the Kurds, accompanied us for hours on our way.

The rest of our journey to Aintab was now plane-sailing. The road was tolerable and the traffic such as gave evidence of some degree of commercial activity. We counted over 1200 camels laden with merchandise which we passed in one day.

Aintab is a town of some 20,000 inhabitants, and they are made up of Greek and Armenian Christians and Kurdish Mohammedans in about equal numbers. It is the capital of the Syrian vilayet, and is situated on the River Sadjur, a tributary of the Euphrates. Like Biredschik, Aintab includes an old mountain fortress, which was already known at the time of the Crusades—when it was taken by Saladin, and again in the year 1400 by Timur the Tartar. To-day it is the seat of wool and cotton manufactures, a commercial depot of leather, cloth, honey, and tobacco.

At Aintab we changed our mode of travelling for the last time; for we disposed of our saddle-horses and proceeded to the coast in the same type of tumble-down conveyance as that in which we left Trebizond. Dr. Hepworth was very sorry to part with his sure-footed little grey mount, which had carried him from Bitlis without a single mishap or stumble. Altogether our experience of the Anatolian horse was one to be remembered with gratitude: never seeming to tire, tractable, docile, and sure-footed as a goat, this breed of horse, which is to be found throughout the Turkish Empire, is truly a friend of man. It is the only horse I have ever known which stands at the bidding of its master for hours together without being tied up. Also, I never once saw a horse treated unkindly during the whole of our journey.

The monotony of riding day by day on horseback at a snail's pace for weeks in silence, from early dawn till sunset, over an endless succession of undulating roadless hills and vales, with occasional spells of dreadful jolting in springless carts and carriages, had told on our spirits. Thus we all had good cause to rejoice over our arrival at Alexandretta. The sight of the sea once more, as from a high ridge of hills we first beheld the blue waters of the Mediterranean, after passing nearly two months in a wild, almost treeless and pathless country, was a thrilling sensation. Cut off from all the comforts of civilization, which lifelong usage causes us to take as a matter of course, their true value came home to us. Dr. Hepworth involuntarily recalled the famous episode in Xenophon's "Retreat of the Ten Thousand" where the Greeks at last greeted the sea—in their case, the Black Sea—with the cry: "Thalassa! Thalassa!"

Here, for the first time since leaving Trebizond, we beheld an inn. We were shown into a bedroom and were delighted to see what we had gone without for so long, and thus learned to appreciate as a luxury—a bed, a water-jug, a washing-basin, a table, and a chair.

Founded by Alexander the Great, Alexandretta is picturesquely situated, but otherwise a poor place, bearing all the signs of Oriental neglect; even the harbour, at which various steamers call, looked deserted and dilapidated. The town itself is surrounded on the land side by swamps, to the fever-breeding character of which the many white gravestones in the large cemetery seemed to offer eloquent testimony, inasmuch as the place has only about 1500 inhabitants. Thus the European colony gives it a wide berth, for its members reside ten miles away in the pleasantly situated town of Beilan. The vegetation, however, is very rich, almost tropical in character: beautiful palms and giant cactus plants flourish in abundance.

In summarizing the incidents of our journey, which had now come to an end, our Hungarian doctor turned to Dr. Hepworth and myself and said: "*Now* that we are well out of it I think we can congratulate each other all round. For I do not mind telling you that there was hardly a day, or rather a night, on this terrible journey in which we were not exposed to the risk of catching smallpox or typhus." At Erzeroum several of us had been vaccinated, by the advice of the British Consul, though it was only with the greatest difficulty that lymph above suspicion was procured in the town.

Another, and by no means a trifling, danger which we luckily escaped was one which had been foretold us in Constantinople as the most serious possibility of our journey, namely, snowstorms and heavy rains producing floods. Had we encountered either of them in an awkward place it might have delayed us for days, even for weeks, in a country without roads or bridges. Fortunately, we met with neither the one nor the other. During the whole eight weeks we were on the road it never rained, and only snowed now and then for short periods.

Shortly after leaving Erzeroum our leader, Sirry Bey, was taken seriously ill with an internal inflammation, which only yielded to the application of ice. On this account we were obliged to remain several days in a village on the road to Bitlis until he got better. But even then he had to be borne between two poles fastened to two horses. But for our Hungarian doctor he would probably have succumbed.

We were obliged to leave our Roumanian interpreter behind us in a hospital at Alexandretta, as he had contracted erysipelas in a Turkish bath at Erzeroum. This complaint developed into an infectious disease of a tuberculous character termed sycosis, which necessitated shaving off all the hair on his body. Thus afflicted he had accompanied us all the way, and we often had to put up with his sleeping on the ground close to us.

After staying a couple of days in Alexandretta and partaking of the hospitality of the United States Vice-Consul we embarked on board a steamer bound for Constantinople. During the uneventful voyage we had ample leisure to review the impressions gained on our expedition, some of which, though they are not free from sundry repetitions, I have jotted down in the following chapter.

CHAPTER VII

SUMMARY OF OUR JOURNEY

Truth is established by investigation and delay;
falsehood prospers by precipitancy.

TACITUS

MARK TWAIN in one of his entertaining books tells us that his travelling party was dirty at Constantinople, dirtier at Damascus, but dirtiest at Jerusalem.

Our party had already obtained the Jerusalemic stage of uncleanliness, and consequent ungodliness, a few days after leaving Erzeroum. We passed through close upon eight hundred miles of country sporadically inhabited by Armenians, still living, however poorly, in the midst of Circassians, Kurds, Arabs, Turcomans, and Turks. We saw them "alive" in their villages. We met them travelling alone along the high road without any escort or arms, the women now and then riding on horseback astride like men. We conversed with innumerable Armenians, priests and bishops of whole districts among the rest, and were assured by them that in such and such a district no outrages, no violence, no molestation whatsoever, even though revolutionists were about, had taken place. Lastly, our Armenian cook rode for hundreds of miles ahead of us quite alone, unarmed, and never encountered the slightest enmity, even far less than he might if he alighted as a stranger on horseback among the miners in some Christian community. And yet these Armenian agitators do not hesitate to assert that the Moslem Turk is bent on the extermination of their race. An even more untenable statement is that the Armenians are a "nation," and as such are entitled to autonomy. The Armenians are not a nation, but an Asiatic race among many other races forming remnants of independent states in olden times. If half, or perhaps three-quarters of a million of Asiatic Armenians, now sporadically distributed over an area half the size of Europe, form a *nation*, what are we to say of the five million Russian Jews cooped up within the pale assigned to them by the Russian Government? Why does not Europe take up their case? What answer would Europe get from Holy Russia if she did so? But this does not exhaust the question. The ethical sentiment of Europe, rightly or wrongly, but in every case armed with enormous power, steps in and says: "Even if these facts are admitted, they do not excuse, much less justify, Turkey in using the means she adopted to crush a rebellion in our enlightened Christian age." Here the Armenians undoubtedly have a very real grievance, which Turkey must see to at once unless her rule is to pass from her in Asia as well as in Europe. But the task will not be an easy one. We need only put ourselves in her place in order to realize its difficulties.

Here is a vast Mohammedan country, the Sovereign of which is acknowledged by international law to be the Sultan of Turkey. This country belonged to the Turks even before the discovery of America. To-day it is honeycombed with Christian, mostly Protestant, missionary schools, the avowed object of which is to educate a small Christian minority—be it admitted the most thrifty, shrewd, pushing, and intriguing of all Eastern races—in the Christian religion and at the same time in modern European ideas, and to bid them look to the Western world outside Turkey as their natural protector. This was bound to make these Asiatics discontented with their Asiatic status. It is denied that proselytism in any form was attempted or intended. I was informed by an American missionary at Bitlis, who had lived thirty years in Turkey, that formerly there was only one small Protestant Armenian sect in the whole of Armenia, and this was in the little town of Hunuesch, between Erzeroum and Bitlis. Yet statistics show that the pupils of the 621 Protestant schools distributed throughout Asiatic Turkey in 1896 numbered 27,000. Thus, whether proselytism has been intended or attempted, or not, it has, *de facto*, taken place on a large scale, for the existence of 27,000 Protestants, school pupils constantly renewed with each succeeding generation, out of a total Armenian population of half to three-quarters of a million (say a million if you will),[9] represents a preponderant percentage of Protestants among them. These are not views, but facts, which can be easily verified, and with regard to which the reader may draw his own conclusions.

> 9. According to Cuinet, the number of Armenians in the Turkish Empire some years ago was 1,144,000, of which about two-thirds would fall to Asiatic Turkey proper; whereas in Russian Transcaucasia there were said to be nearly 1,000,000 Armenians, and about 100,000 in Persia. The Armenians are thus scarcely more numerous in Asiatic Turkey than the Italians and Belgians in France, distributed over a country twice the size of France.

I met missionaries everywhere in Turkey. I was in their houses as far west as Macedonia, and as far east as Bitlis, near Lake Van, on the frontier of Persia. They nearly all evinced a marked anxiety not to be held responsible, however remotely or indirectly, for the revolutionary movement in Turkey, which in its turn was the source of the massacres that took place, and I willingly believe that they never really intended to provoke disturbance or encourage rebellion against the Turkish authorities. Still there cannot be any doubt that their teaching—not their doctrines, perhaps—had the result, probably never intended, and one it has taken a couple of generations to attain, of fostering the Armenian revolutionary movement throughout Asiatic Turkey.

Everything had been carefully prepared in Asia and in the Press of Europe and America before the Armenian outbreak to boom a second Bulgaria. The project failed because, as compared with the years 1876–77, Liberalism as an aggressively agitating force happened to be under an eclipse in Europe in 1895–96. Asiatic Turkey is honeycombed with European and United States Consuls. These gentlemen occupy a quasi-diplomatic status, although in some places there are next to no national interests to be protected.[10] Their dragomans and servants are mostly Armenians. When these Consuls walk abroad, accompanied by their armed bodyguard, it is as superior beings, as petty Ambassadors. They are entitled to address the Turkish Governor-Generals with almost Ambassadorial authority. They report the outcome of their investigations to their Ambassador at Constantinople, who thereupon proceeds to examine and cross-examine the Turkish Government at the Sublime Porte on the basis of the Consul's communications. This activity was at work long before the outbreak of the Armenian massacres, and yet there are still people who are surprised if the Turks do not seem to love the Christians. Imagine the great towns in England, or the United States, or France, or Germany favoured by the presence of Moslem Consuls walking abroad like Ambassadors, with extra-territorial immunities, present in every law court, and reporting every petty larceny that takes place to their Ambassador! What would be the feelings in the above Christian countries towards these Moslem Consuls?

> 10. American interests in Anatolia are mainly those of the missionary establishments, schools, hospitals, workshops, etc.

The English Vice-Consul at Bitlis read us some extracts from his latest report to Constantinople. They consisted of a number of incidents of petty wrongs regarding internal administration in Turkey—arbitrary enforcement of local dues, petty larceny among Turks or what not—matters mostly reported to him by his Armenian dragoman.

"But are not these purely internal local concerns?" I queried.

"Yes, to be sure," was the reply.

"Well," I rejoined, "if you are hereafter appointed to a Consular post in Russia, and you make similar reports to the British Ambassador at St. Petersburg, and the Russians find it out, don't you think you would run a fair chance of the Russians making your official position rather uncomfortable for you?"

"I fancy I should," was his jocular reply.

Incidents such as this show the vexations which the Turks have had to put up with in their own country at the hands of the Christians. Some time ago an English Consular official in Persia wrote an article on Persian administration in an English magazine, with the result that the Shah of Persia successfully insisted that he should not return to Teheran.

To these petty vexations must be added the more serious trouble Turkey has constantly to reckon with in consequence of the peculiar attitude of the Russian Government in regard to the Armenian revolutionary movement. We have been witnesses in our time of the vast resources of the Russian Government when called upon to deal with their own revolutionary parties. If the Russian Armenians would like to put them to the test they need only try to force the Russian Government to cease interfering with their schools, their language, and their creed. They might then indeed discover for themselves what a Russian millstone is like. But no!—they submit to Russian tyranny, preferring to organize revolutionary work at Kars, Tiflis, and Batoum directed against Turkey; and "helpless" Russian bureaucracy avows its inability to discover, much less to interfere with such!

The problem to be faced by Turkey is to ensure that security of life and property in her Asiatic dominions which is a *sine qua non* with every Government, be it under the Crescent or the Cross. The Kurds must be forced to give up their predatory propensities. They still defy the Valis, and are, I was credibly assured, now and then secretly encouraged in this by the military commanders, who intrigue against the civil authorities, and it is difficult for the Government in Constantinople to ascertain the true facts of the case. Shortly after our journey the Modiki Kurds slew the kaimakan of Modiki and along with him eight Turkish officers. They were still unpunished a year afterwards.[11] And yet if such men cannot be brought to respect the law, and security for life and property be assured, it will shortly be said of Asiatic Turkey as it was of ancient Carthage: "Delenda est Carthago." The Kurd, like Zola's hero in "La Débâcle," must take to the plough and work. It is the law of the Universe; not even a Khalif can exonerate his subjects from its inexorable working. Turkey is in need of reforms—nor is she the only country in need of them. This is admitted on all hands. And among these none are so vitally necessary as those of an economic nature. It is a misfortune for Turkey to-day that Mohammed lived practically in a desert, where trees and roads were few and far between. If this great reformer had lived, for instance, in Anatolia or Mesopotamia, one of his earnest injunctions to his followers would doubtless have been that every one of the Faithful should consider it to be his duty to plant a tree and assist in making public roads, the latter being the occupation which Goethe tells us finally brought contentment to the restless soul of Faust. The Mohammedans, who after twelve hundred years still religiously obey every injunction of their Prophet, down to the number of prayers and ablutions to be said and practised per diem, would have naturally carried out his wishes in this particular. And, if so, Asiatic Turkey would wear a very different aspect from what it does to-day. Alas! those who have travelled through Turkey in Asia and witnessed the absolute lack of roads, bridges, and almost every other civilized convenience which marks a certain mean level of social organization, can only come to the conclusion that the Turk is more or less of a nomad: a nomad horseman, as he was a thousand years ago, leading the life of a nomad, even though his predatory instincts are now and then dormant, and, when exercised, are impartially put into practice at the expense of both the Mohammedan and the Christian.

> 11. At the moment of preparing these pages for the press, sixteen years after my journey through Asiatic Turkey, I learn from several independent sources that although no recrudescence of the massacres has taken place, the conditions prevailing there to-day are even more unsatisfactory than of yore. The Imperial authority under the régime of the Young Turks is at a lower ebb even than in Abdul Hamid's time. In addition thereto must be reckoned the dreadful losses in human life caused by the wars in Tripoli and the Balkans, so that the fields are now largely tilled by women and old men.

The American mind is said to be able to find the shortest and straightest road from one given point—logical or material—to another. The Englishman may possibly come next to the American in this; the German is slower, but he is infallible in the long run, for he works a problem out stolidly with the assistance of logarithms and trigonometry. As you near the East, the capacity for discovering the short, straight, logical line decreases—the Austro-Hungarian finds it sometimes, the Turk hardly ever.

This constitutional inability to seize the value of an established fact or series of facts, and to draw the obvious logical conclusion therefrom, has all along hampered the Turk in putting his case before the world, even in instances where seven out of ten points were in his favour. I have heard an educated Turk cite the case of an Armenian tailor who had deserted his wife and run away with another woman as a proof of the iniquity of that interesting race. In his lack of logic the Turk recalls the Swiss woman who appealed to the court for a divorce from her husband. On being asked what grounds she could advance in support, she replied after thinking awhile: "He is not the father of my last child."

Individual Americans, Englishmen, Germans—yes, even English missionaries—will now and then make out a better case for Turkey than all the Turks put together with whom I conversed during my several prolonged visits to Turkey.

"Yes, you must remember this question has two sides. There is a deal to be said for the Turks; the Armenians are not all angels," an American missionary said to me in Anatolia. "For, let there be no mistake about it, it is only the

Pharisee who bids us fancy that the priests of Baal have erected altars exclusively among the Turks."

I contend that the responsibility for the horrors which took place in Asia Minor rested in the first instance with the Armenian revolutionists who instigated them, and not with the Turks, who are an Asiatic people like the Russians and the Persians, and whose methods of repression are not very different from theirs. The Armenian revolutionists were responsible for the suffering of the innocent for the guilty. I have read their pamphlets, their stirring circulars urging the helpless Armenian hamal (porter), peasant, and artisan to rise and throw off the Turkish yoke. These documents were only too often ruthless and indefensible in their unbridled lawlessness. The Armenian revolutionists stated that it was impossible to hope for anything but persecution *on religious grounds* from the Turk. Now the Armenian language, creed, and schools are perfectly free in Turkey, whereas they have always been persistently interfered with in Russia. The Armenians accuse the Turk of persecuting Christians, whereas the high road from Trebizond to Erzeroum, as already stated, is dotted with Christian monasteries and churches unmolested during centuries.

Our steamer stopped at Mersina, Rhodes, and Smyrna on our way, but we landed only at the last-named place. In strolling through the city, we took our farewell of Asiatic life with its caravans and its camels—a long line of which met us in the street. Our arrival at Constantinople took place after sunset, and in observance of some queer harbour regulations we were obliged to pass the night on board, being allowed to disembark only in the morning.

Before leaving for Paris we stayed a few days at Constantinople. The Sultan sent word asking me to draw up a report of the impressions gained on our journey. This I did, and expressed myself to the effect that what had made the deepest impression on us was the lack of roads, bridges, and trees, and the desolate nature of the whole country, some parts being little better than a wilderness. There would seem to be a great field for beneficent work in these lands.

Thereupon the Sultan expressed a wish that Dr. Hepworth and myself should come up to the Palace and be received by him. After duly considering the matter, we replied jointly that, as His Majesty had asked us to render a service to truth and justice by our investigations in his Asiatic dominions, we thought it best to leave Constantinople without seeing him; for, if we were received in audience, it would get known and might be construed into our having only acted as his agents—a surmise which would certainly discount the value of Dr. Hepworth's impartial account of our experiences. The Sultan seemed to recognize the force of our contention, for he sent us a kindly message embodying his best wishes for our journey, and expressing the hope that we might some day come again to Constantinople. In order once for all to dispose of the idle rumours which were current at the time, I may add that neither Dr. Hepworth nor myself accepted any memento or present whatsoever from the Sultan. A decoration which His Majesty subsequently sent to Paris for Mrs. Hepworth was returned through the proprietor of the *New York Herald*.

Before leaving I received the following letter from Munir Pasha:

PALAIS IMPÉRIAL DE YILDIZ, CABINET DU GRAND MAÎTRE DES CÉRÉMONIES.

"CHER MONSIEUR WHITMAN,

"Je vous envoie par le porteur une lettre que j'ai écrite à l'adresse de Monsieur Gordon Bennett, et qui est relative à votre récent voyage en Anatolie.

"En vous priant de vouloir bien faire parvenir cette missive à sa destination, je me plais à vous dire combien je me félicite des relations personnelles que j'ai eu l'honneur d'avoir avec vous, et à vous assurer du bon souvenir que je garderai de ces relations.

"Votre dévoué,

"MUNIR."

LUNDI, *12 Janvier 1898*.

Most of us can recall the peculiar sensation we experience on returning into the fresh air from the fetid atmosphere of an ill-ventilated apartment, the noxious nature of which we had scarcely realized as long as we remained there. So also the true character of Eastern conditions only seemed to come home to us after we had left the country. At least, speaking for my travelling companion and myself, we only seemed to realize the treeless desolation, the wilderness of roadless Kurdistan, as we were passing through that beautiful, richly verdured section of Austria and South Germany traversed by the Orient Express. Then it was that the contrast enabled us to appreciate as perhaps never before the benefits of the high state of European land culture. The same feeling might well suggest itself to the traveller in passing from Dover to London through Kent, the Garden of England. On arrival in London, however, other features of Eastern life forced themselves on our memory and suggested comparisons less flattering to our own social conditions. Needless to say they were those which account for the strange fascination the East exercises even upon some of the most cultured European travellers.

Indeed, it was a strange, for the moment an almost unaccountable, sight to behold the crowds of people flocking into the City of a morning from the suburbs. This haste, this eagerness, as if their very life depended upon catching a train, constantly struck one as unnatural after living for weeks along the banks of the Tigris and the Euphrates, staying in villages in which the conditions were so primitive—a contrast almost beyond comprehension. What could be the driving motive that impelled these people to this feverish activity, this restlessness? Why, hunger, to be sure, the grim necessities of the battle of life, a struggle to be continued without intermission from youth to the grave, and, when done, leaving little to take note of except, perhaps, that a mutton chop more or less would be called for at their particular luncheon haunt. And the background: Tooting Bec, Clapham, and Brixton in the South, Pentonville and Hackney in the North, and the East End with its miles of slums and its paupers; or to take those parts more familiar to middle-class life, Marylebone and Bloomsbury, with their interminable, dull, featureless roads and terraces, the rows of houses in their dread monotony, veritable soul-killing mausoleums of the living; what Ruskin termed "streets in hell." To think of their commonplace residents with their fads and fancies and their sympathies rigorously narrowed down in accordance with the tenets of their faith. All are supposed to worship the selfsame God, and yet they are socially divided, cut off from each other as nowhere people are in the East. Surely life should have some wider and nobler scope, aim, and application than the mere gratification of the appetite to live, were it only to cultivate that restful spirit without which any earnest self-communion, any deeper philosophy of life is an impossibility. At least so it seemed to strike one fresh from two months' intimate communion with Nature—from conditions varying little, I should say, since Abraham's time—a patriarchal state of things which acknowledges a chief, but gives brotherhood, if not equality, to the rest of the community. I had seen men in Syrian villages—the mayor, for instance, a stalwart, full-bearded peasant patriarch of dignified bearing and benevolent mien, in profile not unlike the stone images of the Assyrian kings in the British Museum—slowly rolling cigarettes with refined, beautifully shaped hands. Somehow it was a dignified memory, in spite of the backwardness of the country, lacking in all our scientific and sanitary improvements. I had not come across a single man with grimy hands, and, except in one Armenian village near Bitlis, I had not seen a woman or child in such rags as I often see in London. Much less had I heard of cases of starvation, nor was I told of forlorn, painted harlots or drunken women—surely items worth recording on the credit side against much that is to be deplored and commiserated with.

Some months after my return to London I received the following letter from the companion of my Armenian hardships:

NEW YORK,

April 22, 1898.

"My dear Whitman,

"I was glad to see your familiar handwriting again, and almost thought I could hear your voice.

"Yes, my dear fellow, those were troublous, but still good, times; and now that I have largely forgotten the hardships, I should like to do something of the same kind again. I did get the letters you sent, and thanked you for sending them. Did my letter miscarry? I fear so, as you did not acknowledge the receipt or answer my questions. Did you say your article was in the April number of *Harper's*? I have sent for it, and am sure that I shall have great pleasure in reading it.

"I worked hard at my book[12] while in Paris, then went to Marseilles, to Nice and Mentone. The book is now nearly finished. It will cover about three hundred pages, possibly more, and will be published in September. I shall take pride in sending you a copy.

"My health is good. I am still a bit nervous, but that is because I have not yet rested as I ought to have done. The summer I guess will see me right again. You do not tell me about yourself. What are you doing? Where have you gone, or do you expect to go to Berlin[13] as we thought? Moreover, do you expect to write a book? This is important, for it is sure to be a good one. You can do it, and you ought to.

"Please give my regards to your good wife, and believe me,

"Always yours,

"George H. Hepworth."

> 12. "Through Armenia on Horseback," by the Rev. George H. Hepworth. New York and London, 1898.

> 13. Reference to an offer made me by the proprietor of the *New York Herald* to go to Berlin as its permanent correspondent, which I declined.

Nearly seven years elapsed before circumstances took me back for a short visit to Constantinople. This time I went no longer as the representative of a great newspaper, but only as a private individual. All the greater was the surprise I felt on my arrival to find a warm welcome from the friends I had previously made there. From the Sultan and his entourage down to the kafedji, who used to hand me my cup of coffee in the Palace, and the swarthy arabadji, whose black stallions took me on my daily round of visits, they all seemed to bear one in kindly memory in gratitude for what they deemed were services rendered to their country, and this too, after a lapse of seven long years, in the Mohammedan East! This has often struck me as extraordinary in an age in which a lifetime of beneficent work, even when recognized at all, is forgotten in a week.

In the remaining chapters I have striven to reconstruct under different headings the impressions and experiences gained during my various visits to Turkey.

PART II

CHAPTER VIII

YILDIZ

The Spider hangs the curtain over princely palaces,

The Owl stands sentry on the cupola of Efrasiab.

SAADI, *Gulistan* (Persian)

Baluk bashdan kokar.

(Turkish Proverb)[14]

> 14. "The fish begins to rot at the head."

THE circumstances already related under which I went to Constantinople made me a frequent visitor at the Imperial Palace of Yildiz. The so-called Palace (recently dismantled) consisted of an extensive stretch of park-land surrounded by high walls in which were fair gardens, woodlands, lakes, interspersed with different buildings of the most varied types and kinds. There were mansions, country-houses, stables, stud establishments, military barracks, a theatre—even a zoological garden and a china factory being thrown into the hotch-potch. Several thousand people were gathered here, consisting of the members of the Sultan's family, their separate establishments and their dependents, besides a horde of Palace officials of every imaginable type and denomination.

During thirty years the Sultan of Turkey directed, single-handed, the destinies of his Empire from this place, paralysing every other authority, the official channels of Government included; working as hard as any nigger, yet with chaos in the end.

On a warm summer day there was an element of repose about the surroundings of the Palace soothing to the jaded nerves of the Western European, and quite different from what fancy would conjure up in connexion with the spiritual head of three hundred millions of human beings. A solitary Albanian soldier stood on guard at the entrance of the Palace, close to which on either side were unpretentious-looking porters' lodges, whose inmates, without any uniform or other distinctive mark of their responsible position, asked you your business. If your face was known to them and a small douceur quickened their memory, you passed through without any further ado. If not, a polite request for your card and a query as to whom you wished to see might bring the request to wait whilst inquiry was made. Or it might be that merely giving the name of some influential official would suffice and you were allowed to proceed on your way.

On passing the porter's lodge into the wall-surrounded precincts of Yildiz and turning to the left, the eye was arrested by a low-lying, bungalow-like building in which a staff was employed to peruse a promiscuous mass of European newspapers, and to translate extracts which were deemed suitable for submission to the Sultan. In the same building the stock of the various Turkish decorations was kept in a cupboard, to which, as occasion arose, the officials would come and take out those that might be wanted for bestowal.

Immediately in front of you was another building of a similar, though superior, type. Here the ground floor was devoted to the offices of the Grand Master of Ceremonies; on the first floor was that of the Sultan's First Secretary, Tahsim Pasha. You passed on to the right towards a slight incline, up which many a fat Turk has toiled breathless, and beheld further to the right a more pretentious and massive structure in that peculiar bastard Oriental style of French design which apparently came into fashion in Turkey in Abdul Aziz's time, and which, on a larger scale, is represented on the European shores of the Bosphorus by the palaces of Dolma-Baghtchè and Tcheragan, and on the Asiatic side by Begler-Bey, the villa farther away, in which once upon a time the Empress Eugénie had been the Sultan's guest. In this particular building, in the Palace at Yildiz, Ghazi Osman Pasha had his office and several of the Sultan's chamberlains had their rooms. There also the sittings of the Supreme Military Commission, over which Osman Pasha presided, were occasionally held.

Immediately on the left was another white structure, with a richly ornamented glass door in the centre. This was the Sultan's own kiosk, where he was much during the day and where he granted audiences. Rarely was a soldier, or indeed any other person, to be seen there, for the military guard-house was hidden from view farther away to the right. There a solitary soldier stood on guard, and the chances were that a stray officer would be sitting on a camp-stool close by smoking a cigarette. But no challenge came as you passed on to enter another unpretentious two-storied bungalow type of building. A number of dirty goloshes in the hall denoted that the official residing here must be a personage who had many callers and was much sought after, and no wonder! It was the office of the notorious Izzet Pasha, the Sultan's Second Secretary, his favourite, and reputed to be the most influential personage in the Turkish Empire. You walk upstairs and take a seat in his room, where already a number of persons are awaiting his arrival—indeed, several rooms are full of callers waiting to see him.

A cat moves along the corridor rubbing its sides against the wall. Nobody thinks of disturbing it. Izzet Pasha's little son is playing about the room. The white buildings of Constantinople are seen in the distance from the window, indistinct in the mist rising from the blue waters of the Bosphorus on a sunny morning. A few pigeons coo and play on the leads immediately under the window. Undisturbed, they too are apparently safe from intrusion. In the garden immediately in front some gardeners are peacefully at work. In the room itself a Turk takes a small rug which had lain rolled up in a corner and places it on the floor so that at the further end it is supposed to point in the direction of Mecca. Thereon he murmurs his prayers. Only his lips move, at times almost convulsively. He kneels down, bends backwards and forwards, repeatedly bringing his forehead down into contact with the carpet; he folds his hands on his breast, then rises upright and stretches them out with palms upward. This continues for fifteen or twenty minutes, and nobody takes the least notice of him or his proceedings. Then he picks up the rug, folds it carelessly, throws it into a corner of the room, and begins talking unconcernedly with those present. "Il a fait ses prières, il a fait son devoir," and within five minutes he is as blithe as the rest of the company.

We are still waiting, for one and all are anxious to have a few words with the powerful favourite. He is expected, but he has not arrived yet, and, as far as any distinct obligation to put in an appearance is concerned, may not appear at all this day or the next. For among the possibilities of his position is that of having fallen into temporary disgrace overnight and being ordered like some naughty school-boy to stay at home and not to quit his konak for days together. Sometimes he would not leave the Palace at all, but work half through the night, for which eventuality a bedstead stood in one of the waiting-rooms. On this particular occasion he has been attending an important meeting of the Conseil des Ministres—a Cabinet Council, we should say—at the Sublime Porte in Stamboul. He is already on his way to Yildiz, leaning back in his closed brougham, for he is not popular, and consequently not anxious to be recognized. His carriage has thundered across the rickety old wooden planks of the Galata Bridge, he has driven along the shores of the Bosphorus, past the arsenal, Tophanè, past the Palace of Dolma-Baghtchè, and is now driving up the steep hill from Beschiktasch towards the Palace at a sharp trot. The heavy gilt harness of the two magnificent black carriage horses gleams in the sun as the white foam starts from their coat. It is as if instinct had revealed to the very walls that the great man is coming, for everybody is on the alert; even the cat in the corridor, still rubbing its sides against the wall, curls up its tail higher than before in purring glee. I look out of the window, and am just in time to see Izzet's slim figure coming through the narrow passage at the back of the building. He is surrounded by several secretaries and attendants and followed by a crowd of suppliants, who are anxious to interview him and put their claims before him even before he has reached his sanctum. There is a rush to the door, and half a dozen dark-eyed servants simultaneously offer their services to divest the great man of his overcoat. He takes his seat at his desk, upon which lies a heap of letters. They have arrived overnight, most of them addressed in Turkish characters, but one of stout dimensions has a boldly printed address in Latin characters to his Excellency scrupulously enumerating all his titles and dignities. It is from the Deutsche Bank in Berlin, where he keeps his banking account, and through which institution he invests his securities—the harvest of the favours bestowed upon him by his master, the sum of which, according to rumour, is a private fortune of several millions. He bows distantly to those present and goes through the stately Turkish salute, termed "temena," to each one in turn of the visitors who are seated on the couches or all round the room, and who return his greeting with the same dignified motion of hands and head, though with an extra degree of deferential eagerness. He hands cigarettes round, and even throws some across the room to one or two of his more familiarly known visitors, and then proceeds to open the most important of his letters. Coffee is brought in, smoking is indulged in, and there is a distinct air of relief and ease among those present; but still not a word is spoken.

A fine, dignified-looking man in the prime of life, wearing the garb of a Sheikh or a Ulema or Mollah, crosses the room and takes a seat quite close to Izzet Pasha. He is evidently a personage of importance, for the two converse a long time in whispers, and whereas the Sultan's favourite is most courteous to his interlocutor, the latter maintains a dignified, almost severe demeanour. As I was told afterwards, he is one of the most influential of Ulemas in Constantinople, learned in law, and of high standing as regards personal character. Izzet assured me that this man was able to trace his descent from Mohammed, if not even back to Abraham. He enjoys high consideration in the Mohammedan world, beyond that of any pasha or even the Grand Vizier himself. There is an evident reflex of his high standing in the deference with which Izzet listens to what he has to say, and with good reason, for the chances are that he will remain a great personage in Turkey long after the favourite has fallen into disgrace or the Sultan himself has passed away. The men of this type are among the most distinguished visitors at Yildiz—these Sheikhs, Mollahs, and Ulemas, who, in their white and green turbans and flowing garments, come occasionally from distant parts of the Turkish dominions and look in to have a chat with the Sultan's Second Secretary, by whom they are treated with greater distinction than any other visitor. They are in fact the only callers with regard to whom the word deference can justly be used; for they are almost the only visitors who do not come to ask for personal favours. They stand for the ideals of conduct of the Mohammedan world.

As the sunflower turns naturally towards the sun, so also every hope of worldly advantage, every hope of preferment, turned at that time towards the Imperial Palace of Yildiz and the august person of the Sultan. Only those who have had personal experience of the conditions prevailing at this centre of intrigue can form a conception of what is conveyed in so simple a statement. The prestige of being in Imperial favour could raise the humblest to a position of influence over and above the Grand Vizier himself, not to mention such minor satellites as Ambassadors or Ministers of State. The Turkish Ambassador on leave might be obliged to loiter about antechambers for weeks and months together without being admitted to an audience of the Sultan, whereas the favourite would go in and out daily, even hourly. Thus "to be received" was the first stage on the road to fortune; to be granted a favour the second step, the culmination of which lay in the magic word "Iradè," meaning the Imperial decree by which a favour promised and granted, whether a high appointment or a valuable concession, had become law.

Sheikhs, Ulemas, Mollahs, Softas, even the Muezzin of the Minaret (the caller to prayer), Armenian Patriarchs, Archbishops, Archimandrites, Grand Rabbis, Ministers-Plenipotentiary, Turkish Ambassadors awaiting their final instructions, Pashas, Generals, Admirals, Ministers, were to be met here doing antechamber service and sitting round the room in silence for hours, even days together. I have even met here a deputation of Kurdish chiefs of the Milli tribe, with Ibrahim Pasha, their leader, a right jovial fellow, and as mild-mannered a man as ever cut a throat, whose advent at Constantinople with a regiment of Hamidiè cavalry shortly after the Armenian outbreak caused quite a panic among the nervous members of the foreign colony in Constantinople.

Traders called for their accounts and sat down sipping coffee with the rest: imagine the collector of Marshall and Snelgrove or Whiteley walking into Buckingham Palace and sipping tea with one of the King's chamberlains! Officials came begging for their overdue salaries. The Hebrew Court jeweller from Stamboul was a regular caller. One day he brought a beautiful coronet of diamonds and pearls which he drew from a bag, and which Izzet Pasha took in to the Sultan, probably destined as a gift for one of His Majesty's many wives. He too, like the rest, I was told, was unable to do business on a cash basis, the Sultan being in his debt to the amount of some £T20,000 or £T30,000.

Those who are familiar only with the social effulgence, the mystery surrounding Turkish diplomatists abroad, from the full-blown Ambassador accredited to the Great Powers to the Minister-Plenipotentiary and Envoy-Extraordinary, can scarcely form an idea of the everlasting delays, tracasseries, humiliations, and heart-burnings which often preceded their appointment under the Hamidian régime. Sometimes the suspense dragged on for months, and nearly wore out the heart of the suitor for the post. Even more aggravating were the circumstances which followed upon the recall of a diplomatist who might not have satisfied the Sultan. I knew a Minister-Plenipotentiary and Envoy-Extraordinary of distinguished family and high intellectual attainments who, after being summarily recalled from his post, haunted the antechamber of the Sultans secretaries at the Palace for ten years without obtaining another appointment in all that period; nearly half a lifetime wasted in idleness, chewing the bitter cud of hope deferred. No wonder that such a man became disgusted with Hamidian conditions and longed for the introduction of European institutions. "How can you hope to carry on a Government," he once said to me, "which does not even pretend to furnish a Budget?" He was one of many who were great admirers of England, and longed for English influence to regain a foothold in Turkey. The whims of the autocrat, the intrigues of his surroundings, sounded the funeral knell of every form of honesty, as they shut the door to every chance of ability coming to the fore. For all that, such conditions having been more or less traditional features of Oriental life from Byzantine times down to the present day, their effects were less disastrous to the Turks themselves than to some alien elements in the service of the Sultan; upon these they acted in some cases like fire and sword, extirpating the last vestige of self-respect.

Solicitants for favours of every kind—place, office, appointment, contributions in money—used to swarm into the Palace. The applicants embraced nearly every nationality that was represented at Constantinople, with the one, and I cannot help saying striking, exception of Russia. Whatever may be averred in connexion with bribery and corruption, official or otherwise, in Russia itself, or of the ruthless policy towards the Ottoman Empire pursued by Russia for generations past, I can say that during my many visits to Constantinople I never met a single Russian either at the Palace or elsewhere asking anything of the Turk, and the Russians are the only nation of which I can say as much; for even the Americans were not above seeking favours in the missionary interest. The only Russian I ever knew to call at Yildiz was the chief dragoman of the Russian Embassy, M. Maximow. It was during the Armenian trouble, and he came to rage and threaten. "Go in to your master and tell him to go to ...!" he shouted, to the dismay of the stately Turks present, whose voices never rose above a whisper in the hallowed precincts of the Palace.

Those unfamiliar with the Turkish character can scarcely form an idea of the importance attached by the Turk, and more particularly the ex-Sultan, to the power of the pen—the eagerness with which the expression of European public opinion used to be scrutinized by the authorities in Abdul Hamid's time under a régime which was popularly supposed to be carried on in open defiance of the spirit of the age. One of the means by which those eager to curry favour with the authorities sought to gain their object used to be to defend the Sultan in the Press. At times a ray of naive humour would mingle in the game. Thus, on one occasion, a pasha of my acquaintance had taken up the cudgels and written a dissertation in defence of the Sultan's claim to the Khalifate. He may have thought that he had thereby given proof of his zeal, and perhaps even expected some recognition in return. What was his surprise, after receiving a curt summons to appear at the Palace, to be met in a cool manner by one of the Sultan's secretaries. The latter took him aside and, pointing to the sun which shone through the window, said: "You see the sun? Well, there it is! No argument is necessary to prove its existence. So it is with the Khalifate of the Sultan. It needs no demonstration, no defence. His Majesty does not wish you to write about the Khalifate any more."

The Sultan's extreme sensitiveness to European newspaper opinion afforded a wide scope for intrigue at the Palace, inasmuch as Abdul Hamid attached exaggerated importance to newspaper articles the relative value of which he had no means of verifying. This idiosyncrasy was traded upon by a cohort of adventurers of different nationalities, some of them of most shady antecedents. They were supplied with funds in return for their supposed influence with the Press in England, France, and Germany. Some were paid a fixed salary by the Sultan; others were fed by occasional doles from his different favourites, acting on the supposition that they—the favourites in question—would be credited with the effusions of these minions as proofs of their own zeal in the interests of his Imperial Majesty. Rarely could Oriental astuteness be found together with such childlike gullibility as was evident in this connexion. The representative of a powerful journal would be snubbed, whilst the correspondent of some obscure sheet would be extravagantly rewarded for some supposed service rendered to the cause of Islam. It has been stated that European newspapers were regularly subsidized by the Palace; but, except in the case of an obscure periodical, *L'Orient*, which appeared in Paris, and a Vienna compilation of news items drawn from telegraphic agencies and called the *Courrier de L'Est*, I never met with any tangible evidence in support of this assertion.

Another feature of lavish expenditure was connected with the Ramadan festival. On this occasion every official at the Palace, including all the pashas in Constantinople, received an extra month's salary, which amounted to about one hundred and fifty thousand Turkish pounds. It was sometimes necessary to borrow this amount from one of the banks or to withdraw it from the funds of the customs. The more one saw of this state of things, the easier it was to understand the eternal impecuniosity at the Palace, and the more one wondered how the Sultan ever managed to make both ends meet.

Towards mid-day an endless stream of Turkish visitors, fat and lean intermingled, dressed in the black frock-coat termed stambolin, could be seen toiling up the hill in the broiling sun to partake of the hospitality indiscriminately offered to the thousands feasting daily at the Sultan's expense.

Some of the parasites of the Palace used to be on the look-out to be sent by the Sultan "en mission spéciale" on some quixotic errand, at times of a rather undignified nature. Lavish expenses were allowed in the shape of a little bag of gold, and if successful there were chances besides of subsequent preferment. The case of a Field-Marshal who was sent to Berlin to engage a cook for the Sultan has occupied the Berlin courts of law since the deposition of Abdul Hamid. I recollect an engineer of the Hedjas Railway returning from Budapest, whither he had been sent on a similar errand on behalf of a pasha. The latter introduced this official to me with the words: "Il est Juif de race, Allemand par nationalité, et Turc par son emploi."

An amusing feature of life at the Yildiz Palace was the arrival of a certain military element on the scene whenever there was a chance of baksheesh or preferment. The poem in Heine's "Buch der Lieder" comes to mind in which he depicts himself as being a god and distributing largess broadcast, causing champagne to flow in the streets:

The poets to such festive treats

Pour in a happy flutter!

The ensigns and the subalterns

Lick clean both street and gutter.

The ensigns and the subalterns—

Now aren't these fellows clever?—

Feel sure a miracle like this

Can't hope to last for ever!

There was something of the comic-opera order, not to say of Christmas pantomime, in this feature of life at the Palace. The transformation scene in "Cinderella" is not more kaleidoscopic in its changes. The obscure little pill-man, once happy at home in his strenuous vocation, passing his evenings in a beer-house, is suddenly called to Constantinople and driven about in a carriage and pair, dressed in a Turkish uniform "made in Germany," with a jewelled bauble dangling from his collar. Just as suddenly the carriage and its black horses are gone, and the worthy doctor has to appeal to the law courts of Berlin for the salary owing to him by the dethroned Sultan.

Bobadil Pasha, Bombastes, Swashbuckler Pasha, Boule-qui-Roule Pasha (a French importation who was said to have owed his successful career to the sirenical attractions of Madame Boule-qui-Roule), Birra (beer) Pasha from the Fatherland—one and all of them enter upon the scene, play their little parts, and disappear through the trap-door exactly as in a pantomime. Alexander of Battenberg, the Prince of Bulgaria, is presented with an Arab steed by the Sultan, but goes away without it, for Marshal Bombastes, the Master of the Horse, who was entrusted with the task of its delivery, had lost or otherwise disposed of it. There were some truculent personages among these gentry.

Calling one day on Ibrahim Pasha, who had succeeded the late Munir Pasha as Grand Master of Ceremonies and Introducer of Ambassadors, I saw a tall, pompous personage in the uniform of a Turkish General engaged in conversation with his Excellency. To judge by appearances he was a very Bobadil, a swashbuckler sort of man, one of the grasping, cunning windbag variety which Abdul Hamid's promiscuous generosity tempted from the barrack-room of his native country to a palace on the Bosphorus, to the dismay and disgust of many a loyal Turkish heart. Six feet of coloured cloth surmounted by an almost round bullet head, bobbing up and down mechanically as if set in motion by wires, the features of the man were commonplace, if not downright plebeian. A hectoring, flamboyant mien stamped the whole personage, breathing the soldier's contempt for the civilian, which is one of the most ominous phenomena of contemporary Europe. And yet he was by no means one calculated to inspire fear: the sort of man that an American cowboy would throw out of a bar-room without taking his pipe out of his mouth.

Vorne mit Trompetenschall

Ritt der General Feldmarschall

Herr Quintilius Varus.[15]

> 15. "Full in front with trumpet blast
> Rode Field-Marshal General
> Herr Quintilius Varus."
> (German Student Song)

I took a seat, awaiting my turn to approach his Excellency, and, as is customary, bowed right and left in doing so. The tall man drew himself up and seemed to resent the courtesy of a mere civilian. But what particularly attracted my attention was that he pestered Ibrahim Pasha with details, given in execrable French, about the ailments of his wife, whom he had recently conveyed to a European sanatorium. It was a sight to note the courtly patience with which Ibrahim Pasha listened to the narrative of Miles Gloriosus, for it is the very worst form of breeding in the eyes of a Turk to refer to one's womenkind. This edifying tête-à-tête went on for some time. At last pomposity was about to take his leave. I held up a newspaper in front of me so as to spare him the trouble of making up his mind whether he was to notice me on quitting the apartment or not. Ibrahim Pasha accompanied his visitor to the door of the ante-room leading out of the building. It was a most amusing sight as I peered over the newspaper through the open door. I saw the two engaged in conversation, the loquacious officer indulging in lively gesticulations. On Ibrahim Pasha returning to the room I said to him: "If I might venture to put it to your Excellency, I would be prepared to wager that the pasha who has just left the room gave way to an impulse of effeminate curiosity and asked you who I am."

"Yes, to be sure he did," Ibrahim Pasha smilingly replied. "But I did not gratify him. I merely told him that you were an American." "Well then," I rejoined, "if he should ever ask you the same question again, pray tell him, with my compliments, that my name is perhaps better known than his own in the country of his birth."

The sun shines through the window and lights up the faces of the grave, swarthy-featured Turks. Officers in full dress, decked out in all their stars and sashes, are pouring into the Palace, for it is Friday. The Sultan has had a good night. Everything is *couleur de rose*, and the Palace officials are getting ready for the Selamlik. Izzet Pasha divests himself of his black frock-coat with the help of a dark manservant, and dons a gorgeous gold brocaded and wadded uniform covered with Turkish and German decorations, doubling the size of his little, attenuated Syrian figure. There was something almost childlike about it all in its contrast to the grim realities of life. The diplomatic loggia was filling. Some of the foreign Ambassadors, eager *de faire acte de présence*, were rarely absent on such occasions and would bring some officers of their respective nationalities to see the show. These had generally just arrived at Constantinople, with a keen scent for favours which would be showered upon them after the ceremony in the shape of commanderships of the Medjediè or Osmaniè Order, for an inferior class of which a poor Turkish officer might wait a lifetime in vain.

The great Officers of State, the Grand Master of Artillery, the fat Minister of War, the Minister of Marine, a little humpback, a notorious personage, and the rest of the pashas—military and civil—are all gathered together in the inner courtyard of the Palace in anticipation of the Sultan starting for the Selamlik ceremony. A military band is heard in the distance. It is playing the "Hamidiè March," composed in honour of His Majesty, a somewhat thin and commonplace production. And here I may mention a fact which is not generally known, that military bands as such are quite a modern feature in Europe, and owe their origin to the Janissaries. "Janitscharenmusik" is still to this day the term used in Germany for an infernal din of tin kettles, pipes, and brass. To the Turk, then, is due all the noise which has become such a public nuisance in our time on the continent of Europe; a heavy responsibility before the tribunal of decency and decorum!

We crane our necks, looking towards the left, when from the rising ground we see the military pageant coming along: first of all the Ortogrul Cavalry, followed by the Sultan's Albanian Guard, trained to the mechanical Prussian goose-step, singularly out of character with the whole bearing and appearance of these untamed sons of the Albanian hills. Then the Sultan himself appears and drives past in an open carriage, with Ghazi Osman Pasha, the hero of Plevna, sitting opposite him.

The Sultan alights, enters the Hamidiè Mosque, and the muezzin from the top of the adjacent minaret calls the Faithful to prayer. An interval of about half an hour follows, in which tea and cigarettes are served to the Sultan's guests. At last a slight stir is noticeable at the entrance of the mosque. The Sultan reappears, enters an open victoria, the reins of which he handles himself, and drives back to the Palace up the hill, followed by a throng of gaudily attired functionaries—old, white-bearded men among them—running after the carriage as best they may: a somewhat undignified sight to a European.

Listen: [MP3] [MIDI]

Music XML: [MusicXML]

Musescore: [MuseScore]

The band now strikes up the Austrian "Double-Eagle March." It is almost imperative to have heard the famous trio of this most enthralling of military marches—a languorous, sensual theme—in order to gain an idea of the effect a military band is capable of producing upon a susceptible crowd. The popularity of the "Double-Eagle March" throughout Austria-Hungary and the German Empire has long been general. Composed by a bandmaster of an Austrian regiment, it has been set to music in close upon twenty different arrangements. A great deal of what is incomprehensible to strangers in latter-day Germany may be attributed to the effect of this popular military march on the public, and, what is more, on those who are supposed to influence and inspire it. If there is a march in the whole world which produces intoxication without either alcohol or hashish, it is this one.

A parallel to the last years of the Second Empire and Jacques Offenbach's Grande Duchesse de Gerolstein, General Boum-Boum, and Prince Paul would suggest itself on the occasions when foreign princes and princesses with their hungry retinues came to visit the Sultan. The Prince Imperial would find his counterpart in the Sultan's poor little sons, who got on horseback and figured in the pageantry of the Selamlik. It is a wonder that there were still some quiet nooks in which a philosophic contemplation of the vanity of things could be indulged.

One day, now long ago, I paid a call on Munir Pasha at his office after the Selamlik. I have already had occasion to mention this high-bred, gracious, and kind Turkish gentleman. Not a breath of scandal, slander, or concession-mongering ever touched this man, whose influential position during many years might have brought him wealth for the mere asking.

"How are you to-day, my dear pasha?" I asked, as he came beaming with kindliness towards me, shaking hands in European fashion, a form of greeting rarely indulged in by the Turk. "Ah, mon cher!" he replied, as a hamal (porter) passed in front of the window, carrying a dinner tray on his head, "you see that poor fellow! How gladly would I exchange with him, and hand him over all my forty-two Grand Cordons into the bargain, if he could only give me his lusty health in return." Munir Pasha was a martyr to asthma, and before my next visit to Constantinople he had passed away.

CHAPTER IX

SULTAN ABDUL HAMID

I come to bury Cæsar, not to praise him.

The evil that men do lives after them;

The good is oft interred with their bones.

SHAKESPEARE, *Julius Cæsar*

SO much has been said and written to the detriment of the ex-Sultan Abdul Hamid that it would seem to be an almost hopeless task to break a lance in his favour; and yet to do so, at least with regard to the human aspect of his character, is nothing more than a bare act of justice.

As he timidly peeps out of the window of his palatial prison at Begler-Bey, on the Asiatic side of the Bosphorus, he has now ample leisure to reflect on the ingratitude of those he loaded with his favours.

Time hath a wallet at his back

Wherein he puts alms for oblivion,

A great-sized monster of ingratitude.

And if he be familiar with the history of his own time, in bemoaning the unhappy fate of his country he may well re-echo the bitter words of the Austrian ex-Emperor Ferdinand, who, living in retirement at Prague when, in 1866, the victorious Prussians appeared before the city, exclaimed: "Surely it was scarcely worth while to force me to abdicate in order to bring things to their present pass!"

Certain figures have come down to us as typical of the extremes of fortune, and some are identified with Constantinople; of these that of Belisarius, the victorious general of the Byzantine Emperor Justinian, lies nearest. After great deeds of war, he is said to have ended his days in a prison, through the iron bars of which he implored the charity of passers-by: "Give, oh, give an obolus unto Belisarius, whom virtue had raised and envy has brought so low."

The ex-Sultan Abdul Hamid offers the latest instance of a similar change of fortune, for on his deposition an orgy of vilification was let loose in the Press of the Old World concerning this unfortunate Sovereign, who only a short time ago was able to boast the friendship of Emperors. One of the last to be entertained by him was a daughter of the House of Habsburg, upon whom, as was customary with him, he poured a rain of diamonds. To-day all these visitors have departed, and the ex-Khalif of the Faithful has not a friend left in the world among the crowd of high, well, and Imperial born to whom, in his prosperity, he played the part of a generous host, and upon whom he squandered countless millions of treasure in one form or another, either as presents or in expensive entertainment. Between them and him constant relays of highly paid emissaries were flitting on confidential missions along the iron roads of Eastern Europe, always at his expense. Close upon 4000 parasites were daily remorselessly draining his financial resources by living on him, and the more lavishly he dispensed his favours the deeper became the morass of ingratitude which at last engulfed him. But even this record does not exhaust the list of his iniquities. He was said to have hoarded fifty millions, whether in francs or pounds sterling matters little, which he invested in German banks. And it was these millions which excited the cupidity of his conquerors, and upon which they were bent on laying hungry hands.

"The power of kings is based upon the reason and folly of the people, but more upon their folly. The greatest and most important thing in the world has human weakness as its basis; and this very basis is admirably secure; for nothing is more certain than the fact that the people are weak. That which is founded on reason alone is badly founded, as, for instance, the recognition of wisdom."[16]

16. Pascal's "Pensées."

This may serve to explain much in connexion with those exotics of our democratic age—the autocrats, and more particularly the career of the ex-Sultan Abdul Hamid, though the lesson conveyed is not applicable to him alone, even among the living. Autocrats can have little or no conception of real values; whilst their system makes it next to impossible for them to train those whose abilities and knowledge of realities might be of use to them.

The career of Abdul Hamid offers too many parallels to that of Napoleon III not to call for notice, embodying as they well may a useful lesson to those who care to understand. Abdul Hamid wanted to monopolize power, and in the end everything slipped from his grasp.

I had not been long in Constantinople when it occurred to me that public opinion, as in the case of Napoleon III, overrated the Sultan's ability and his knowledge of mankind, and underrated his qualities of heart. It was not so much the disastrous results of his reign to Turkey which irresistibly forced this conclusion upon me as the poor estimate one could not help forming of his surroundings and of the exaggerated importance he attached to things and individuals of questionable value; notably those complimentary missions and visits the practical results of which stand revealed to us to-day in all their futility. The Sultan was imbued with the instincts of a gentleman in his personal dealings, and these inclined him to accept as sincere assurances of friendship from those whom he thought in a position to be as good as their word. And yet I have it on fairly good authority that the only true friend in high station the Sultan possessed was the Emperor of Russia, who promised him that he would not undertake anything against Turkey during his reign, and kept his promise. On one occasion I ventured to point out to Baron Marschall von Bieberstein that the never-ending visits of foreign princes and the expense of their extravagant entertainment,[17] whilst the salaries of the officers in the Army remained unpaid, were calculated to make the Sultan unpopular with his own people. He replied that His Majesty could never have enough visits of that kind. The Sultan clamoured for them, and, as we know, he got an ample supply of what he clamoured for.

> 17. The Turkish deputation which the Sultan sent to greet the German Emperor in 1908, at Corfu, was said at the time, in the German newspapers, to have cost him, one way or the other, £T35,000.

When Abdul Hamid ascended the throne, the internal situation of Turkey was so critical that it required a man of great strength of character not to lose heart. The tragic circumstances connected with the death of Abdul Aziz had contributed to unhinge the mind of His Majesty's brother, his immediate predecessor. The reckless extravagance of Sultan Abdul Aziz and his Court had left the finances of the Empire in hopeless embarrassment. The Ottoman Empire was practically bankrupt. Corruption reigned supreme in every department of the State. The governorships of the provinces had frequently been sold at enormous prices to men who were utterly corrupt and unfitted for their positions, and who oppressed the unfortunate populations under their charge, extorting from them, often by torture, the profits of their industry. Justice was shamelessly bought and sold in the courts. There was no uniform system of taxation: every governor fixed his own tariff and enforced its collection, however unjust and oppressive it might be.

The responsibility imposed upon a young and inexperienced prince was heavy indeed; for Abdul Hamid was only thirty-four years of age when he succeeded to the throne, which was still reeking with the blood of his predecessor. Disorder reigned in the provinces. Bosnia, Herzegovina, Servia, Bulgaria, and Montenegro were in open rebellion, and, incited by Russia, declared war against Turkey. The demands of the States practically amounted to independence and autonomy. Russia backed up their demands by moving a corps d'armée to the banks of the Pruth, and declared war. What followed is part of the history of the nineteenth century.

It affords strong testimony to the firmness of the Sultan's character that he did not despair: far from it. From the very first, Abdul Hamid boldly grasped the nettle of sovereignty, and for thirty years never ceased for a day to devote his whole energies to the task of ruling his country. As a stray indication of such devotion to duty, it may be mentioned that during all that period he missed only one Friday's public visit to the Hamidiè Mosque for the ceremony of the Selamlik, and that omission was due to illness. Surely this is almost a unique record of regularity of habit, and one which only a constitution fortified by a life of constant hard work and studied moderation could have rendered possible.

To-day it is no empty assertion to say that Abdul Hamid endeavoured to be the Educator of his people. He had hardly girded on the sword of Ejoub, the emblem of Turkish sovereignty, when he sent an aide-de-camp to a German professor living in Constantinople Dr. Mordtmann and sought his assistance to organize the so-called *Mekteb Milkiè*, a school for training Government Civil officials. He established the Turkish University at Haidar Pasha, near the English cemetery at Scutari, at an expense of close upon £1,000,000. The water supply of Constantinople, the finest in the world, is due to him. Constantinople had abundant fresh water at a time when Europe had little or no idea of its hygienic value. Under Sultan Suleyman there were 700 fountains or springs in Constantinople. Most of these had been allowed to dry up and decay. One of Abdul Hamid's first acts was to create a gratuitous supply of fresh water for the inhabitants of Pera at a cost of £100,000.

In former days, famine and hunger-typhus, which invariably accompanies it, periodically ravaged Asia Minor. Anatolia now exports wheat worth two million pounds per annum and is growing cotton, and Angora produces improved cereals which are used in brewing and are also exported. Turkey even exports goats' skins so far as it can do so in face of Russia's prohibitive tariff. When Abdul Hamid came to the throne Constantinople lived on Russian beef; an excellent quality is now raised in Anatolia which is sent to Constantinople by rail.

It must be borne in mind that these and other achievements were carried out in the face of constant money difficulties. The Sultan founded technical schools and hospitals and made roads and railways. But more remarkable still, from a Turkish point of view, were his manifold efforts to raise the status of the Turkish woman. He even created a special decoration for ladies, the Order of the Chefakat. He was a true Mohammedan in his democratic breadth of sympathies, and there can be no doubt that in his early days he was honestly intent on the recognition of individual worth and character.

Where so much power is placed in the hands of one man, it goes without saying that abject servility has to be reckoned with; nor is this a feature peculiar to Turkey. That the Sultan often showed respect for unwelcome though honest opinion is, under the circumstances, a merit which calls for recognition. That he did so in early years is attested by some well-authenticated facts. He had hardly come to the throne when he decided to call a Council of State to judge the conduct of Midhat Pasha and his associates, who had agitated for the introduction of European representative institutions into Turkey. The question was submitted to the Council, which sat at the Imperial Palace, whether the said persons were guilty of treason or not. All the members but one brought in a verdict of "Guilty." The single dissentient vote of "Not guilty" was given by Emin Bey, a German—a native of Mecklenburg—who had entered the Turkish service and embraced Islam. His colleagues, in their dismay, pointed to a curtain in the apartment and endeavoured to convey to the recalcitrant German that the Sultan was posted behind it and consequently cognizant of his opposition to the vote of the rest. Emin Bey, however, remained firm, for he belonged to the old school, and added that he could not conscientiously decide otherwise. Every member of the Council received some mark of the Sultan's favour, but the highest distinction of all was reserved for Emin Bey.

Either the Sultan must have been endowed with remarkable qualities, or circumstances must have been exceptionally favourable to him, or both, to have enabled him to hold on during thirty-two years, in the course of which the pay of his soldiers was always in arrear and the gang of favourites at the Palace was constantly plundering him. Whatever may have been the effects of despotic rule on his character in the course of years, there can be no doubt that when he came to the throne he was filled with a high conception of the responsibilities of his position. It is established beyond question that it was with the greatest reluctance he consented to his brother being deposed, and then only after the most reliable medical opinion regarding the latter's mental unfitness had been taken. At the beginning he endeavoured to attract honest advisers to his service.

But whatever may have been his qualifications or shortcomings as a politician, there can be little doubt that he possessed many unusual personal attributes, though perhaps of a negative nature. He had the calmness, the reticence, the self-control of a well-bred man, never proffering advice and not given to expansiveness, for his nature was undemonstrative. He showed no vulgarity, no coarseness, no hectoring or bullying. He had no desire to put himself forward, to be communicative, his thoughts in the market-place, nor was he carried away by the shouts of a crowd or intoxicated by its homage. When on a Friday he passed in front of the cheering troops his features always bore an expression of calm dignity and benevolence, and a marked capacity for leniency and forgiveness. His recognition, even to the humblest, for services, many of a trivial kind, was extreme.

Abdul Hamid's political ability has been for long an article of faith, even with those who were prepared to deny him every other quality, and the results obtained by him during a period of over thirty years in his dealings with the Great Powers, freely admitting that their final outcome was a negative one, point undeniably to his having been endowed with some political gifts. He must have possessed a certain inborn sagacity, which, however, was not nurtured by a wise bringing up or such an experience of the world as would have enabled him to gain an insight into real values, notably in the selection of high-class character. This handicapped him through life. It showed itself in his misplaced confidence, as evidenced by the rise of many favourites of doubtful character from absolute obscurity to power and great wealth, and it does not tell in favour of the common belief in the Sultan's perspicacity that so many of those he distinguished were mediocrities even when they were not rogues.

Professor Vambéry relates the following incident as an illustration of the queer type of men that managed to gain the favour of Abdul Hamid: "Among these obscure worshippers round the Sultan was the famous Lufti Aga, in his official capacity of Master of the Robes, but in reality the most intimate confidant of the Sultan, in spite of his Turkish origin.[18] I had a rather curious adventure with this worthy. One day whilst walking with the Sultan in the garden I saw this man approaching His Majesty, and looking closer into his face, I recognized in him the servant of Mahmud Nedim Pasha, formerly Grand Vizier, distinguished by his Russian sympathies—hence his nickname, Nedimoff—in whose house in Bebek I acted formerly as teacher of French to his son-in-law, Rifat Bey. In accosting the said former servant somewhat boldly I noticed a perplexity on his face, but still more remarkable was the blushing of the Sultan, who asked me whether I knew his favourite man before. 'Of course,' said I, 'Lufti was a servant in the house of Mahmud Nedim Pasha, and he often cleaned my boots.' Tableau! The most intimate man of the Sultan a shoeblack by origin. But this intermezzo did not disconcert Abdul Hamid, for Lufti went on in his delicate service until the end of his life. Such is the East, and such are Orientals, however so much gifted."

> 18. This refers to the Sultan's well-known preference for Albanians, Circassians, and Arabs. Izzet Pasha was an Arab.

We have only to review the course of affairs since his deposition to be forced to the conclusion that whatever Abdul Hamid's mistakes may have been, he was yet able to postpone the catastrophe which, under any circumstances, must now be admitted to have been inevitable in the long run.

To-day there can be no doubt that he was more or less driven into the arms of Germany by the attitude of England both under Mr. Gladstone and in a less degree under Lord Salisbury, more particularly during the period known as that of the Armenian atrocities. But even this should not have sufficed to endow him with the faith he undoubtedly possessed, where only the cleverness to take advantage of Germany's assistance in a utilitarian spirit would have been justified. This credulity on his part was all the more remarkable seeing that it was never shared by the more sterling and astute political and religious elements around him. These never swerved in their preference for England and the English, even in the darkest days which followed upon the Armenian massacres in 1895 and 1896. They still held on to the Turkish traditions of the Crimean war of friendship between Turkey and England. In departing therefrom the Sultan may be said to have made the exchange familiar to us as children in Aladdin's story of bartering old lamps for new. England's goodwill was Turkey's old lamp in spite of every misunderstanding.

In some respects the ex-Sultan shone to advantage as compared with many rulers of the past and some of the present. Notably was this the case as regards his sense of gratitude for services rendered and of loyalty to those who he believed had served him well. My own sporadic relations with His Majesty have furnished me with evidence that his wish to benefit others could even outweigh a consideration for his own interests. For supposing that my position as correspondent of the *New York Herald* at Constantinople was really of any value to him, as he plainly believed to be the case, his proposal to me to leave that paper and enter his service was obviously contrary to his own interests. The guiding principle of others in the Sultan's position would have been to continue to utilize a man's services at no cost to themselves and then to throw him over. How different was Abdul Hamid's conduct in this as in so many other cases! The late Mr. Whittaker, for many years correspondent of the *Times* at Constantinople, received signal marks of favour at the Sultan's hands, in spite of the anti-Turkish attitude of that paper. He was, I think, acceptable to the Sultan as a man of culture and a talented musician, and was now and then asked to come up to the Palace to play the piano. When a rupture finally took place, it came about through Mr. Whittaker himself, who was exasperated at the restrictions placed by the Censor upon the *Levant Herald*, of which he was the proprietor.

Barely has a sovereign distinguished a private individual, without wealth or rank, and a foreigner into the bargain, with his intimacy to such a degree as the Sultan did in the case of Professor Arminius Vambéry, whom he used to address by the familiar, almost endearing, term of "Baba." This friendship had its source in his appreciation of the Professor's distinction as an Oriental scholar and his well-known sympathies with Turkey, her people, and her religion. Here, again, the estrangement was, I believe, due to the Professor himself, who became dissatisfied with His Majesty's political tendencies, which he could not see his way to share or champion.[19]

> 19. See Appendix, pp. 287–288.

The Sultan possessed a rare delicacy of feeling, which he now and then showed in small things, doubly remarkable in a man in his exalted position and, moreover, always overburdened with work. Thus when Sirry Bey, one of the Sultan's secretaries, accompanied us as chief of our expedition through Anatolia, and was taken seriously ill between Erzeroum and Bitlis, the Sultan was apprised of the fact. He was most anxious to keep the news away from Sirry Bey's wife, and made a point of sending to his konak from time to time with cheering news and a present of money, for fear the Bey's salary might not have been paid to his family in his absence through the ordinary channels. In conferring the Order of the Chefakat on a lady, he caused the following words to be inscribed in the brevet: "Sa Majesté Impériale accorde cette décoration à Madame X pour faire plaisir à son mari." It seemed to afford him gratification to give pleasure to others.

Comparatively few people are aware of the refined nature of one so much maligned; and yet testimony to this effect rests on irrefragable evidence. I need only mention the Sultan's intense love of music, his munificent remuneration of artistes who had been asked to perform at the Palace, and the deep interest he took in Nature, whether animals, birds, or flowers. One day the Turkish Ambassador in London asked me to assist him to procure a book dealing with Australian birds. The Sultan had heard that such a work existed and would like to have a copy. All this may well lead us to inquire how such facts are to be reconciled with the popular conception of his treachery, his blood-guiltiness? The answer is self-evident.

The Sultan was anxiously bent on keeping in touch with the happenings in the outside world. Thus, in addition to reading translations of foreign newspaper articles, he looked through several English illustrated weeklies regularly, the letterpress of which was translated into Turkish expressly for him by his secretaries. One of the first questions he would ask a visitor, after the usual inquiry regarding his welfare, would be concerning some important current event: what might be the outcome of the Russo-Japanese war, the Russian revolution (1905–6), etc. On one occasion he expressed his belief to me that both the Mohammedans and the Jews would outlast the Christian world.

I have often seen it stated in print that the Sultan wore an habitual look of melancholy—in other words, that his main characteristics were sadness and nervousness. Neither my own experience, nor the testimony of others best in a position to form a reliable opinion, bears this out, although the tragic circumstances under which, very much against his will, he came to the throne may well have left their impress on his mind. The Sultan was of an exceedingly sensitive nature. He was a man in whom the domestic affections were very strong; thus a blow, such as the loss of a daughter, might well have had a cruel effect on him, as only those can understand who have loved and lost children of their own. But I do not believe that the Sultan's temperament was one of habitual melancholy. On the contrary, I know that His Majesty could enjoy a joke as heartily as ever did Martin Luther; though the nature of some of the doughty Reformer's sallies would hardly have suited the refined taste of the Khalif of the Mohammedans.

The Sultan on one occasion was inquiring of one of his confidants about a stranger whose personality interested him. His Majesty's informant told him that the individual in question was never seen in coffee-houses or theatres, much less in places of doubtful repute or in suspicious company; that he was most moderate, even abstemious, in his habits; that he sat at home working most of his time, and if he went out, it was to visit a mosque and watch the Faithful at prayer. "Truly a remarkable man," broke in the Sultan; "he might almost be an Osmanli" (for among themselves the Turks never use the word "Turks"). The other, feeling that he had drawn an impossible picture of perfection, which might perhaps encounter the Sultan's incredulity, here rejoined that truth compelled him to confess to His Majesty that he had seen the stranger walk up and down in his room during the hot weather with next to no clothing on—almost naked. This caused the Sultan to burst out laughing. On such occasions—and they were by no means rare—when the Sultan was in good spirits, the monarch's merriment, as if by magic, was reflected in his surroundings. I have seen all Yildiz in the best of good humour, for the word had gone round that "Sa Majesté est de fort bonne humeur," and the news spread far and wide; it even found expression in the broad grin of the hamal who carried the fat pasha's dinner-tray from the Imperial kitchen on his head.

It would, indeed, be no cause for wonder if the Sultan had been occasionally in a serious mood. There are other monarchs besides the Sultan whose humour is not always *couleur de rose*. "Uneasy lies the head that wears a crown" is not a Mohammedan proverb. But the Sultan's strength of purpose, his truly phenomenal powers of work, his abstinence from every form of nervous stimulant except an occasional cigarette and a cup of coffee, are irreconcilable with the idea that he could have been of a morbidly nervous disposition. As to the Sultan's working habits, I have known him to be at work at five in the morning and at that hour keep going a whole staff of secretaries, who had slept overnight on couches in the rooms in the Palace in which they habitually worked. Munir Pasha once said to me: "There is one characteristic of His Majesty which conveys a lesson to us all: it is his extraordinary self-control—his impressive calm. It is almost sublime—no contrariety, no trial seems to ruffle his perfect self-possession. It is truly marvellous."

Making every allowance for the enthusiasm of a devoted servant and a prince of courtiers, I am yet inclined to believe, on the strength of other evidence, as well as from my own personal observation, that Munir Pasha's estimate of his master's nerve was by no means exaggerated. Certain Ambassadors, who had abundant opportunity of testing the Sultan's self-control, might, if they were still among the living and inclined to make revelations of incidents in which they did not come off with flying colours, give even better corroborative evidence than I am able to do.

It has been said that the Sultan was constantly surrounded by a fierce soldiery armed to the teeth, and that sudden death awaited the hapless creature who should venture to intrude unbidden within the sacred precincts of the Imperial Palace. As a matter of fact I doubt whether there is any other palace into which it would be so easy for a stranger to penetrate as it was into the Yildiz Kiosk. All sorts and conditions of men—but no women—used to find their way in and out. As already mentioned, I have known the Pera shopkeeper of English nationality enter the Palace and walk unbidden into the sanctum of the Sultan's all-powerful secretary, take his seat among the Ambassadors, Pashas, and Ministers, sip his coffee and smoke his cigarette, and sit there for hours together as if "to the manner born." So much for the exclusive character of the Sultan's Palace.

I remember more than once being at the Palace rather late in the evening. Everybody had gone home long since. A few servants, wearing fezes and dressed in the black stambolin frock-coat, stood silently in the hall which adjoined the Imperial apartment. Otherwise not a soul, much less an armed man, was to be seen until you passed the sentry at the gate of exit. Nor, indeed, was a sound to be heard on the beautiful moonlight night, except the splashing of the water of the marble fountain, which issued from one of the side walls of the unpretentious one-storied wing. The Sultan was within, hard at work with his secretary in a suite of apartments opposite those of Ghazi Osman. A stranger might have remained there unmolested, as I did in front of the Sultan's room, without a soldier to be seen, or a policeman to call upon him to "move on."

It will always remain a strange feature connected with the dethronement of the Sultan that it came on a sudden, quite unexpected even by those who ought to have been in a position to form a correct estimate of what was going on. As a matter of fact the Sultan's authority was being undermined some time before the catastrophe really took place. He no longer ventured as of yore to act in direct opposition to the advice of his Ministers by granting valuable concessions to his favourites. The pressure of foreign Ambassadors, notably Baron Marschall von Bieberstein, also became more embarrassing.

About this time the Turkish Ambassador at Madrid, Izzet Fuad Pasha, a grandson of the renowned Grand Vizier Fuad, published a book severely criticizing the conduct of Turkish affairs as embodying so many lost opportunities. He was recalled to Constantinople, put under surveillance in the Pera Palace Hotel, and forbidden to leave it even for an airing. Crowds of spies surrounded the hotel by day and by night. Of even greater significance were the doings of Fehim Pasha and his arraignment and disgrace, of which more later. The contradiction between the Sultan's supposed diplomatic astuteness and the short-sightedness which appears to have marked his measures in meeting the forces which were destined to overthrow him has not yet found an explanation.

The personal appearance of the Sultan has been described by many writers, for no monarch in the world was seen so regularly in public as he. Anybody who wished to see him had only to walk up to the Imperial Palace, the Yildiz Kiosk ("Tent of the Stars"), on a Friday morning, and he was absolutely certain of seeing His Majesty as he drove in an open victoria, with Ghazi Osman sitting opposite him, out of the Palace gates to the Hamidiè Mosque to prayer, and half an hour later, on his way back, when he himself handled the ribbons. It is quite true that the road was double-lined with soldiers, but that in no way prevented the spectator from taking stock at his leisure of the Sultan and all his courtly surroundings. Then, again, a number of rooms adjoining the Palace, overlooking the whole pageant of the Selamlik, were placed by the Sultan at the disposal of foreign visitors and the better classes of Constantinople every Friday, and it used to be—until the last few years, as explained elsewhere—the easiest thing in the world for anybody with a decent coat to his back to obtain a card of admission, and thus, for the short period of one forenoon, to become *de facto* a guest of the Sultan. During the interval, whilst the Sultan was in the Mosque, excellent tea and sometimes, on exceptional occasions, even sweets and cigarettes were handed round to the visitors, whilst bags of bonbons were distributed among the crowd in the road on Mohammed's birthday; a list of those present was also regularly handed to the Sultan, who perused it, and if any name was familiar to him, he would send his personal greeting to the visitor in question. Thus the privilege of witnessing the ceremony of the Selamlik from the rooms set apart for the purpose was one involving the acceptance of His Majesty's hospitality. There every Turk appeared dressed in his best, wearing his decorations. This was not always realized by visitors of the English-speaking world, some of whom I have seen in flannel shirts, dirty shoes, and knickerbockers mingling, with complete self-possession, among diplomatists and others belonging to good society, who were carefully attired for the occasion.

The favourable impression which the Sultan is universally admitted to have produced on those who were privileged to come into contact with him was doubtless due to that charm of manner, that quiet dignity which is more or less characteristic of all well-bred Turks. But in his case it was supplemented by a kindly smile and an unusually sympathetic voice, the tones of which conveyed a pleasant impression even to the stranger who was unable to understand what His Majesty had said until it had been translated by the interpreter. The Sultan usually gave audiences on Friday after the ceremony of the Selamlik, when he wore a Turkish general's uniform with the star of the Imtiaz Order in brilliants hung from his neck. As he sat in front of you, his hands resting on the hilt of his sword before him, and spoke to Munir Pasha in his quiet, dignified way, you could not resist the impression of a picturesque dignity. I have also seen him attired in a black frock-coat, cut in Turkish fashion, which just hid a white waistcoat with a gold watch-chain, scarcely differing in appearance from one of his secretaries or the other officials. The only other jewellery was a plain gold ring on the little finger of the right hand with a fair-sized cut ruby, or polished en cabochon. He received his visitors standing. It was customary to sit in the presence of the Sultan after being requested to do so; but the native-born Turk sat only on the very edge of the little gilt chair, and folded his arms across his chest, waiting for the Sultan to address him, and then muttered in reply, while bending low, and touching chest, lips, and forehead with the right hand: "Firman Effendemizen" ("Master, thy word is law").

Many might find it difficult to account for the personal popularity of Abdul Hamid in face of the disasters which marked his reign, such as the Russo-Turkish war and the several Armenian risings. The explanation is to be found in the fact that Abdul Hamid represented the ideals of a ruler in the hearts of his people far more than any Sultan since Mahmud II, who ordered the extermination of the Janissaries. How far he deserved this attachment can be estimated only by making due allowance for the retentive memory of the Turks and their traditional attachment to their race and the tenets of their religion. It is impossible to do justice to Abdul Hamid without realizing to what a depth Turkey had sunk under Abdul Aziz. A knowledge of these facts alone enables us to appreciate the reforms which Abdul Hamid introduced, and for which he obtained credit from his subjects, but none at all from the outer world.

Even allowing for these things and the influence which they exercised upon the minds of the Turkish people, it would be difficult to understand how the Sultan maintained despotic sway for thirty years were it not for the realization that the Mohammedan has a different outlook upon the world from that of the other peoples of Europe. Reverence for the past, fidelity to his faith, deep attachment to the traditions of race and creed—these unfashionable virtues are instinctive with him. Abdul Hamid's strength lay in this, that he represented in his own person, at least for a time, the ways of thinking of his people: that his ways were in essence theirs. In this connexion my thoughts ever and again revert to the scene of the Selamlik, when I saw Ghazi Osman Pasha sitting opposite the Sultan in his carriage. Nowhere in the Christian world can I call to mind such an inspiring picture as this of the white-headed old man being demonstratively honoured in public by his Sovereign and revered by the people, although his name will always be identified with one of the greatest catastrophes that ever overtook the Turkish arms in Europe. And yet in the eyes of his master there was no disgrace, only honour, for one who typified in himself all the virtues that belong to Islam. How can one help contrasting the treatment the Turks and their ruler meted out to their defeated champion with that which the ever ungrateful house of Habsburg bestowed upon that gallant soldier Field-Marshal Benedek, the unfortunate Austrian commander at the battle of Sadowa—all his former services, his splendid record in Italy in 1848–49, when the Archduke Albrecht presented him with the sword of his father the Archduke Charles, the victor of Aspern, his prowess in Hungary, his distinguished conduct at the battle of Solferino in the Franco-Italian war of 1859, all wiped out of memory, and he himself disgraced and sent to die of a broken heart in the obscure little town of Gratz.

Blow, blow, thou Winter wind!

Thou art not so unkind

As man's ingratitude.

CHAPTER X

A CITY OF DIPLOMATISTS

O, what a tangled web we weave
When first we practise to deceive.

SCOTT

I HAVE already mentioned that the Turk is accustomed to the vagaries of despots, to the flatteries and servility which they breed. But to be more exact, it should be stated—indeed, it cannot be too often repeated—that Constantinople was the hearth of duplicity, of every form of intrigue, long before the Turks were ever heard of. The Byzantine historian Procopius of Cæsarea, private secretary to Belisarius, has left invaluable testimony to the treacherous atmosphere of Constantinople in the days of the Emperor Justinian and the Empress Theodora. Other historians have also borne witness that these characteristics marked the life of the Court of Byzantium down to the last hour of its existence. With a tradition of over fifteen hundred years to legitimize the term of "Byzantinism" and all it conveys, it is scarcely to be wondered at that Constantinople has always proved a disintegrator of human character, and that only the strongest and the noblest have ever been able to pass unscathed through this fiery furnace of deceit, in which, be it said, the Christian element has shown itself to be a far abler adept than the Mohammedan. Even now, in the twilight of Turkey's fortunes, many may still remain of opinion—so often expressed in the halcyon days of her prosperity—that of all the races that have ever ruled in Constantinople, the Turkish has been the only one noted for its honesty. Indeed, it is an incontrovertible historical fact that the advent of the Turk in Constantinople inaugurated an era of tolerance, till then unknown in those parts. But however this may be, it cannot be gainsaid that Constantinople has witnessed more intrigue than any other capital in the world—Rome excepted—and thus is fitly considered to be the best training-ground for diplomatists; and many are the stories concerning them. One day an Ambassador met a carriage, guarded by a eunuch, containing some ladies of the Sultan's harem. He endeavoured to peep in at the window, when he received a blow across the face from the vigilant eunuch. Great uproar ensued thereupon, and formal complaint was made to the Sultan on the part of the outraged diplomatist. He was received in private audience, and Abdul Hamid listened patiently to the tale of outrage. On its conclusion the Sultan replied: "My dear X, I have gone carefully into the case, and see exactly how it stands. You are a gentleman, therefore you could never have committed such a breach of good manners as that alleged to have taken place; and consequently no eunuch could possibly have presumed to strike you. The whole affair must be the product of your fancy; pray let us dismiss it."

Another Ambassadorial story tells how an august personage—let us call him Prince Florizel—sent word to the Sultan, by the Ambassador at Constantinople of the country to which he belonged, that he intended to make his Imperial Majesty a present of a horse. Now the Sultan already possessed a number of horses, and he was somewhat anxious to find out what sort of animal the Prince had destined for him. If it was to be a racer, or a so-called "Clydesdale," the Sultan had no use for it. The Imperial horse-boxes were built to suit the size of the animals usually kept there; and in order to find room for a racing thoroughbred or a Clydesdale mare, the Sultan would have to enlarge the stable or to make the gift-horse a head shorter in order to find room for it. In this dilemma he sent a trusted servant privately—that is to say, unofficially—to the Ambassador in question, with His Majesty's best compliments. Would his Excellency be kind enough to say what kind of horse it was intended to bestow on him, the accommodation of the Imperial stables being, etc.? Great indignation thereupon on the part of the Ambassador. "This is not the way to treat me; you are not qualified to discuss this matter with me. The proper person is the Sultan's Master of the Horse. Let His Majesty communicate with me through him, or go to ..." The Sultan's trusty servant returned to the Imperial Palace and gave a "truthful" but Orientally diluted version of what had taken place, omitting the Ambassadorial reference to a certain alternative invoked. For an Ambassador is usually supposed to be *persona grata* with the Sovereign to whom he is accredited, and the openly expressed wish that his Imperial Majesty should accept the alternative of being damned would hardly have rendered his presence in Constantinople agreeable to the Sovereign.

The Sultan declined to send his Master of the Horse to the Ambassador, ignored the whole affair, and took no further notice of the offer. When, all the same, the gift-horse arrived, it was received in silence and put in the Imperial stable to get fat and ugly. No acknowledgment of any kind was vouchsafed, either to the Ambassador or those entrusted with the delivery of the horse. And I am told that Prince Florizel, down to the end of his life, when he had become a powerful monarch, esteemed for his tact and courtesy throughout the world, could never understand how it was that the Sultan, than whom no man more courteous and more genuinely appreciative of a kindness existed, should have had nothing to say in return for this particular mark of attention. According to Professor Vambéry, the Sultan subsequently took his revenge on the Ambassador in question by receiving him one bitter winter day in an apartment without a fire, and his Excellency was laid up with a cold for a fortnight.

If men gifted with the acute perceptions, the prescience and tact of an Ambassador have not always been accurate in their judgment of the East, or happy in their dealings with the Sultan, it will readily be believed that men of inferior calibre are often singularly at sea in their opinions and unfortunate in their experiences with the Turk. The keynote of the Turk's bearing is a serene dignity; and a lengthened sojourn in the East has an imperceptible effect on the traveller from the West. The European gets unconsciously accustomed to expect a certain grace of bearing in the humblest, and when he meets a distinguished representative type from his own country—a man who would be the talk of the capital by reason of his wealth, or some one in high station, a law-giver, hereditary or otherwise—the traveller is disenchanted, and says to himself: "Is it possible that this restless, hustling creature is the type of man we look up to at home?"

There have never been any powerful social elements in Constantinople, as in other capitals, to compete with diplomacy. A millionaire banker might be knocked on the head with impunity in the streets of Pera, but the obscure Vice-Consul of a Great Power is sacrosanct. In every case the social as well as the intellectual life of Constantinople, such as it is, is largely made up of and regulated by the staff of the different Embassies, Legations, and Consulates, of which "his Excellency," the full-blown Ambassador, is the supreme embodiment. Behold him as he comes along in all the pomp and circumstance of his high calling! He steps ashore from his richly ornamented caique, he, the cynosure of all beholders, preceded by kavasses, guards, and dragomans dressed in blue, green, red, or purple tunics and gaiters, richly embroidered with gold and silver. He is obsequiously followed by his secretarial staff; deeply impressing the imagination of the crowd as his carriage drives up to the Sublime Porte or the Imperial Palace. Verily, the Ambassador stands as the centrepiece of a world of tinsel and make-believe, the pinnacle of an edifice of decorative glamour; for the reality of power rests with the Press to-day, and an astute Ambassador builds up his reputation by carefully nursing the correspondents of influential newspapers, for the slighted journalist is in a position to give an Ambassador a deal of trouble.

"To have been an Ambassador at Constantinople," one of the most distinguished of them once said to me, "is to have been *somebody*, at least for once in a lifetime. Compared with an Ambassador here, even an Imperial Chancellor, who is continually badgered and bullied by Press and Parliament, is almost a nobody," he added with a self-satisfied smile. The diplomatic light who expressed himself thus was also quite frank in his estimation of the world in which he moved. Potentates he regarded as merely kings on a chess-board, to be separated from their protecting pieces, and, if of opposing colour, to be hustled, circumvented, and checkmated. He declared that he had become satiated with, and quite indifferent to, decorative distinctions.

These had been showered upon him in such profusion that he now only prized those studded with brilliants, "avec de grosses pierres," such as Gortschakoff asked for from Bismarck.

The facilities for telegraphic and postal communication between the different Embassies at Constantinople and their Governments at home have hitherto not been of that perfect kind which reduces an Ambassador in some other countries to the status of a cipher at the end of a wire. Therefore, a wider field was open for personal initiative on the part of an Ambassador there than elsewhere. The complex personality of Abdul Hamid, round whom everything revolved, also afforded until quite recently exceptional scope to the abilities of an Ambassador, and lent great importance to the dragoman service, *i.e.* the man who holds the responsible post of official interpreter to an Embassy. His rôle demanded varied linguistic accomplishments, tact, and a liberal course of diplomatic education. Among the chief dragomans of the Embassies of the Great Powers were to be found some of the ablest, most astute and cultivated of men, particularly Levantines of Italian or Greek origin. The dragomans form so conspicuous a feature of diplomatic life at Constantinople that the Turks declare the souls of those who have passed away in the course of time flit on the waters of the Bosphorus in the bodies of the flocks of birds so often seen skimming the blue waters at sunset.

Like Bucharest—another preparatory school of budding Ambassadors—Constantinople has long been a seminary, a high school for diplomatists of every country. Here it is that uncouth youths, taken raw from the Foreign Office, their hands everlastingly thrust in their pockets, a pipe in their mouth, with slouching gait and pitiable embarrassment, on entering the room of their official superiors come gradually to discard their angularities and are taught to behave themselves in accord with cosmopolitan usage. They are put through their paces, and finally learn to roar in true leonine fashion in the name of their country.

The gaucheries of the young diplomatists might be a theme for ridicule, but I refrain. On one important matter, nevertheless, a word may be said. It would be well if the British Ambassadorial staff were to abandon that hauteur which some of its members are apt to display towards those of their countrymen who visit Constantinople charged with important commercial interests. It is not necessary that a British Ambassador should imitate the policy of those who use their diplomatic position to champion the commercial interests of their country at the expense of higher trusts and higher standards; but it is advisable to avoid the other extreme of ignoring everything and ostentatiously snubbing everybody connected with commerce as beneath the dignity of diplomacy. Yet this has repeatedly been the line of conduct, as it has been that of inclination. For it was only in 1908 that our Embassy first took official notice of the British Chamber of

Commerce at Constantinople and sent a representative to attend its sittings, who probably thought he was demeaning himself in being called upon to do so. This aloofness towards trade interests and their representatives is all the more inexplicable as many of these young men come of families which owe their worldly position to trade, either as bankers, brewers, meat contractors, or even less reputable connexions. Both the Anglo-Saxon and the Teuton take on a most necessary coat of social polish in Constantinople by rubbing against the more subtle and elusive elements of the Levant, the more graceful-mannered Italian or Spaniard and the well-bred Turk, from the "Excellency" down to the caikdji (boatman) of the Bosphorus. "Texas Jack" can go to school here, did go to school, and so profited by tuition received that on his return home he could not reconcile himself to the every-day rough-and-tumble uncouthness of Yankee-land. He had been favourably impressed by the Turks, and they liked him in return, for there was a touch of genuine unspoilt human nature about the man. One winter the Sultan sent and begged his acceptance of a fur coat to keep the cold out. Thereupon a howl went up in the American Press; accusations of graft, bribery, and corruption—not in New York, but in Constantinople! Altogether it may be said that the diplomatists the United States sends to Turkey, even if they may have been somewhat ignorant of diplomacy as a profession, are invariably men of sterling worth and value in themselves, not chosen on account of their family connexions or financial resources. And this is a matter of importance inasmuch as things are apt to vary according to the character of the representative of a country. The well-bred gentleman would naturally inculcate that urbanity of manner and that cultivation of heart and mind which, far more than any other accomplishments, form the true charm of the élite of European society. The Ambassador less happily constituted can hardly fail to leave his mark on his subordinates in a corresponding degree.

A peculiar type of Ambassador is he who arrives on the scene unduly advanced in life, "un peu gaga, ramolli," whose mechanical style of address and response acts like a yawn on his surroundings. There is again the Ambassador who has been sent to Constantinople in order to be got decently out of the way from his own country. He is known to be in the wake of business, and spites the diplomatic world by giving no entertainment beyond a cup of tea, thus saving a good proportion of his salary, but thereby inculcating the habit of economy among a class only too readily given to spend money. It was said of one such that he "stole like a raven," and had become a millionaire since he came to Constantinople. He managed to keep on excellent terms with the wily representative of another great country, and more particularly with certain journalists who might easily have exposed his menées. One of his exploits was to join the representative of another Power in bullying the Sultan and ultimately blackmailing the Turks shamefully, who thus had good reason to hurl their maledictions at his head when he departed.

A pitiable figure of the diplomatic world is the poor Ambassador: one whose private income is unequal to the calls upon his position and whose life is besides bankrupt in happiness. He sits alone in glittering dejection in his beautiful palace, with no money to entertain and no wife to comfort him and cheer his solitude.

Diplomatic Constantinople is exceptional in that an Ambassador and his staff live out of social contact with the nation to which they are accredited, and are thus thrown much more on their own resources—those of their immediate circle and nationality—than anywhere else in Europe. The Embassies form a social centre for those who come under their influence such as is not readily met with elsewhere in European society. I need only mention, as far as England is concerned, the brilliant names of the past, the many references to be found in diplomatic memoirs to such men as Lord Stratford de Redcliffe, Sir Henry Layard, Lord Dufferin, Sir William White, and last, but not least, the late Sir Nicholas O'Conor, all of whom exercised a beneficial influence over those who passed their time of diplomatic apprenticeship under them. Hence the rôle of an Ambassador at Constantinople—and partly that of an Ambassadress as well—is of an educational nature. Many a young attaché has found in the wife of his chief a motherly and sympathetic confidante whose counsel has kept him out of mischief in this dangerous centre of temptation. For the family life of the English diplomatic world in Constantinople has long been an exemplary one: one to look up to. English diplomacy can boast of having always preserved personal integrity, an aloofness from every species of sordid and illegitimate transaction and from all concession-mongering and cadging for favours of any and every description in the Turkish capital. The English Ambassadorial staff has left such dealings severely alone, a course of conduct which has redounded to England's honour in the past; and as it has always been highly appreciated by the best class of Turks, even in the worst days of England's unpopularity at the Palace, it can scarcely fail to redound to her permanent advantage in her dealings with Turkey in the future. For here we have an ideal of conduct worthy of a great nation.

Turkish diplomatists have always been picturesque figures in European society even when their salaries were in arrear; but when they return to Constantinople they are to be pitied. Many of them have been spoiled by their experience in other lands. A few years in the social whirl of Paris, Vienna, Berlin, or London does not improve them: the Mohammedans in particular are apt to acquire undesirable habits and modes of thought. They become imbued with the worldly cunning, the artificiality and insincerity of European fashionable life, with the extravagant homage Europeans pay to social position, so different from the patriarchal instincts of home, and they are consequently disenchanted when they return to Constantinople to find that they are nobodies, mere hangers-on at the Palace, perhaps destined to spend years as suppliants for work. Without private means, accustomed to spend money like water, these officials are in a hopeless plight. Society in London and Paris has deadened every unspoilt interest and ideal. They have become sceptics and cynics. I met one who was the son of a Minister, said to be one of the most notorious personages in Turkey. He quoted Renan and La Rochefoucauld, and would tell you that vanity and egotism are the driving forces of every human action. Such a man finds his countrymen stupid, not "up-to-date." He believes Turkey to be rotten to the core, and if you tell him that you are a philo-Turk he will take you for a rogue who is in the pay of the Palace. Has the Sultan "received" you or not? That is all that interests him about you. And if you ask him what he does to earn a living, he will be quite surprised. He is military attaché of the Ottoman Embassy at X. "Yes, but what are you doing here?" "Oh, I'm on leave." "Yes, but surely not permanently?" "Well, for a year or two."

The lack of a distinctive, dominant national feature which marks intellectual or social life generally at Constantinople extends to the cuisine. There are not half a dozen establishments in the whole city in which the Western European can obtain a meal that in any way satisfies a discriminating palate. Even at the Club de Constantinople the cooking has the irritating, kaleidoscopic, nondescript character of its members; it is of every and of no nationality. It is only at the Cercle d'Orient, the club of the diplomatic world, and at the Embassies that the cuisine has that Parisian foundation to which the epicure can look forward with pleasure. Under such circumstances it is a great treat to be invited by one of the "gros bonnets" of the diplomatic world whose dinners enjoy a well-deserved popularity. It was on such an occasion that, carried away by the excellence of the fare, I ventured to express myself to his Excellency to the following effect. I had noticed that there was not a single member of his Ambassadorial staff who had not been decorated by the Sultan, so I suggested that he might perhaps prevail upon His Majesty to bestow a decoration upon his cook, whose culinary feats appeared to me to constitute an appreciable auxiliary force telling in the scale of his Excellency's many diplomatic triumphs.

Not overwork, but over-eating, late hours, and no exercise constitute the real handicap to longevity in the diplomatic world in Constantinople, for Ambassadorial dinners and dinner-giving go on all the year round, each Embassy in turn inviting the others: "cutlet against cutlet." This means sitting up late. It is almost impossible for the heads of the different Embassies, who are supposed never to take a walk abroad except when preceded by dragomans and kavasses, to indulge in a quiet daily "constitutional" either on foot or on horseback. Such a mode of living requires a tough constitution, and it is not surprising to find that an Ambassador at Constantinople rarely attains a great age.

English and Americans who are enamoured of what has come to be internationally known as "high life," and whose limited means may not admit of their rubbing shoulders with the diplomatic world in Paris or London, cannot do better than take a trip to Constantinople in the height of the winter season of that gay, pleasure-loving city. Furnished with a few decent introductions, the chances are that they will see something of fashionable life without being called upon to make any "frais de représentation"! There is Oriental lavishness in the mode of entertainment. Something of Turkish generosity in the way of hospitality has become engrafted on to the Christian elements, and invitations to Ambassadorial dinners and balls are not beyond the reach of the travelling English who at home have never come nearer to the regions of fashion than South Kensington or Brompton. Should these advantages, however, be unattainable, a stray guinea or two as a subscription to one or other of the various charity balls given by different nationalities in the town will suffice to ensure social contact with the cosmopolitan financial and diplomatic world. These balls under Ambassadorial patronage and presidency are unique, the more so since they take place in the capital of a people which does not dance. Sometimes it is a fancy-costume ball, at other times one in evening dress, with the military and naval attachés of the different Powers in full uniform. Such an entertainment affords a vivid picture of cosmopolitan life, the atmosphere being that of the Levant and endowed with an articulate abandon, obsolete under our more sedate social conditions. To see the guests arrive is a curious sight. A regular pandemonium of shouts, shrieks, and curses proceeds from the Turkish arabadjis lashing their restive steeds as the carriages jostle each other in front of the building. A unique feature of a past age consists of a few old-fashioned sedan-chairs, from which ladies emerge.

Inside, the building swarms with attachés d'ambassade, representative of every imaginable nationality. British, French, Spanish, Italian, German, Russian, Persian, Servian, Roumanian, Bulgarian, Montenegrin, Greek, not to forget the Levantine ruck of no exact nationality, are gathered together here, but no Mohammedan Turks. Such a ball is a rare treat for the dark-eyed Perote débutantes, some of them of mixed Greek blood of great physical beauty. Looking down from a balcony in stucco Mauresque, the whole scene present a rare whirl of colour, life, and excitement, a picture of the vanity and transience of all things: one which recalls the sad exclamation attributed to Xerxes, in crossing from Asia not far from this very spot, that in less than a hundred years not a single soul of all his hosts would be alive.

CHAPTER XI

THE LEVANTINE

The wish—which ages have not yet subdued
In man—to have no master save his mood.

BYRON

YOU come across a queer medley of races, languages, and nationalities in the narrow streets of Pera, somewhat trying to the nerves in its promiscuous incongruity. Almost with a shock you see the name of Pericles over a grocer's shop, Demosthenes over that of a tailor or a barber, and Socrates or Euripides staring you in the face as the name of a bootmaker. Enter a café or brasserie and you find Germans, Austrians, French, Greeks, Italians, and Armenians at one and the same table playing dominoes or tric-trac. One of such a group, to whom I had mentioned that I should go mad if I lived for long in such kaleidoscopic surroundings, retorted: "We are accustomed to it here. Indeed, I should feel depressed unless I could express myself in half a dozen languages before I went to bed. When I get home to-night, I shall converse in Hungarian with my father-in-law, in German with my wife, in Greek with my children, and in English with their governess. And I shall probably wind up by addressing my servants in Roumanian or Turkish."

I have known a Levantine civil pasha married to an Austrian lady whose three-year-old son would prattle in English, German, Greek, and Turkish. Nor am I quite sure that this list of the prodigy's accomplishments is complete. Such polyglot proficiency as is to be met with among the Levantine element is calculated to impress the monolingual Anglo-Saxon; but in the long run it is not without its drawbacks. Never was the saying, "Qui trop embrasse mal étreint," more applicable than here. Listening to superficial, aimless small talk, defectively conveyed in half a dozen different languages, is apt at last to irritate even the most hardened and indulgent listener. For it goes without saying that these are spoken indifferently, and when put to paper written ungrammatically. According to Continental standards of mental culture, the level of the Levantine is not a high one. The artisan class in this as in other respects are, I should say, decidedly superior to their social betters, and lead a healthier life generally. You may meet individual cases of excellent musicians in Pera society; but the gramophone, not to say the French horn, and third-rate French music-hall entertainments more correctly indicate the average taste of the community. I found it impossible to obtain the songs of Schumann or Franz, and only a poor selection of the works of other great composers was to be had in any of the music-shops of Pera.

Whatever taste for belles-lettres may exist partakes of a second-rate French order. The lack of a definite nationality acts unfavourably in the direction of the cultivation of intellectual pursuits, with the possible exception of the Greek colony, which maintains a touch with the literature of ancient Hellas. This defect also shows itself in the nondescript character of the cookery at the principal hotels and restaurants, as already stated.

A strange and wondrous world this, and, what is equally remarkable, a free-and-easy one into the bargain. To all appearances it is Liberty Hall right round the compass. More particularly does this apply to the stranger within the gates. And all are strangers here who by their pseudo-nationality can claim to come under the privileges of the Capitulations which the Sultans, even in the plenitude of their power, tolerantly allowed to continue in force. Strangers pay no taxes either as individuals or as house-owners. It was only quite recently, and with the greatest difficulty, that the Turkish Government succeeded in making foreigners pay a small stamp duty for receipts on bills, etc. There is full liberty to revile the authorities as much as you please, and even now and then to introduce bombs and explosives with the connivance of a certain Great Power. No wonder that the late Sultan was driven in self-defence to keep a huge staff of professional spies in his service.

Nevertheless, there are no police to be seen, and no regulations in force when to close or when to open your business, whatever its nature. If you sit in a café or a brasserie, there is really no valid reason why you should ever get up, unless to go to the hospital, of which there are any number—to die! No boards are to be seen informing you that you will be prosecuted in case of trespass, no walls (except those round the Imperial Palace) to shut out the sight of the beautiful country, which apparently belongs to all alike. Indeed, there seems no reason why the mule-driver with his load of bricks should not unload where he stands and begin to erect a palazzo of his own on the spot, for the land would appear to belong to anybody, to judge by the absence of enclosures. There is also liberty to cheat to your heart's desire and go bankrupt ad libitum. An English financier who had lived in Constantinople for years once told me that the one thing he regretted on leaving the city was the sense of unlimited personal freedom he had enjoyed there.

I used to stroll through narrow streets into which the sun never enters, though in the summer months it may burn the roofs of the houses. You hear loud shouting across the road from an obscure beer-house, and fancy the place is on fire; which would be no joke in such exiguous surroundings. But it is only a few Germans with beaming faces shouting "Hoch! Hoch! Hurrah!" unable to restrain their delight over the excellent beer Herr Kusch provides for his customers and anxious to give an expression to their unbroken fidelity to the German Emperor. Further up the street, peering through a small damp window, you can see a middle-aged man sitting by a lamp writing a letter. He is a grandfather, but in Constantinople this need not clip the wings of amorous fancy. He is writing a passionate letter to an English girl. He has only seen her a couple of times in his life, and will probably never see her again, for she has gone away to Egypt. But he wants to tell her that she is a "houri"—the ideal of his dreams. It can only be in Constantinople that old men indulge in such fancies, and it is wondrous strange how they are received and reciprocated at times. In a beautifully appointed konak on the hill there dwells a haughty beauty, one of the loveliest women in the Empire. She sails into the room and tosses her empty little thoroughbred head in lofty disdain as she passes her Greek servant. But he does not lower his gaze. On the contrary, the flash of his dark eyes betrays that he has no need to do so. There is no impassable gulf here between high and low born, no helot-bred menial race marked with an abject inferiority, physical, mental, and moral, by the ruthless inbreeding of generations. Beneath an outward veneer of self-control there is a deal of the unbridled, unbroken master man of the Middle Ages left in this population. The slums of Constantinople have before now sent forth lovers for queens and wives for emperors. The Greek valet has the same pride in his veins as the more highly placed, for people in his humble station of life, men and women alike, still possess that sense of unsubdued personality the loss of which is one of the dark shadows which cloud our more "civilized" communities. There may be little education or character here in the conventional sense, and not overmuch reliability perhaps in any sense, but there is plenty of unrestrained human nature. This it is which the high-born lady pines and sighs for, and when she leaves Constantinople she will take her Greek servant with her, to while away the time for her and enliven the dreary surroundings of her aristocratic home, for she has grown to loathe the sight of her uninteresting money-grabbing husband with his sordid interests.

Each nationality, except such as belong to the artisan class, keeps more or less to itself in the Turkish capital and has its separate cliques. The English merchant class long resident in Turkey make an exception in associating and occasionally intermingling with the better Greek families. This exclusiveness is partly a result of the insurmountable barrier of language, so that Europeans may live in Constantinople for years without coming into contact with a Turk above the status of an arabadji. My friend Hugo Avellis was an exception to this rule. Few Europeans had mixed more with other nationalities, more especially with Turks of every class, in the course of a residence of thirty years in Constantinople. What he did not know about Constantinople, the habits, customs, and ways of thinking of its inhabitants, was not worth knowing. Many are the pleasant hours I used to spend listening to his stories and gaining information from him on subjects which were far more interesting to me than the dancing or howling dervishes, the gossip of drawing-rooms in Pera, or the intrigues of the Palace or the Embassies.

A German by birth, educated at one of the excellent Berlin classic gymnasia, Avellis, like many of his countrymen, had already become acclimatized in the land of his adoption. He retained, however, an inborn instinct for thoroughness in his vocation, and with this a strong love of literature, mingled with a thoroughly German idealism in its sanest and best acceptation. German thus by thoroughness and intellectual interests, he had become almost a Turk in his humane recognition and love of his fellow-men. "Bravo!" he would impulsively exclaim on hearing of a generous action.

"If you would judge of the fibre of a man," says a French aphorist, "inquire of his dentist." This dictum applies equally to the doctor or surgeon; and my friend's experiences as a member of the Red Cross during the Russo-Turkish campaign gave him rare opportunities for observing the Turk there, where he is seen at his best: in his silence, in his capacity for patient suffering and self-denial. Avellis was present at the siege of Plevna. He saw the harrowing scenes depicted by the brush of Vereschagin, and witnessed the surrender of Ghazi Osman to the Russians. He came to Constantinople after the war, where his business as maker of surgical instruments, together with the practical experience of surgery gained in the field hospitals during the war, brought him from time to time into contact with all classes of the community, from Imperial Princes and Grand Viziers, the present Sultan included, down to the humble water-carrier. Even the mysteries of the harem are not quite hidden from those of his calling. The high-class Turks value a fellow-man independently of his station in life, and often honour him with their confidence, though his social status be far beneath their own. The "medicine man" in particular has often played a great part in Eastern intrigue. Dr. Mavrogeni, the Sultan's physician in the seventies, was not without political influence. He intrigued against the German Ambassador, Count Hatzfeldt, and fell into disgrace in consequence.

Avellis spoke Turkish fluently, though unable to read its written characters. He was a good Latin scholar, and was familiar with both ancient and modern Greek. With the devotion of a Hellenist he loved to quote Homer in both versions. He also spoke French, Russian, English, Roumanian, and Hungarian, his wife being a native of Hungary. With such opportunities and accomplishments he became a rare judge of the Turk and a reliable guide to the intricacies of Oriental life. I see him still in the Passage Oriental, abutting on the Grande Rue de Pera, in his little shop, over the doorway of which a large signboard announced that he was "By Special Appointment Purveyor of Surgical Instruments to his Imperial Majesty the Sultan."

Quite a queer and characteristic nook of Constantinople is this Passage Oriental, in which from early morn is heard the cry of the huckster, the zazavatij, selling vegetables, and, in the autumn, luscious grapes and oranges; the fishmonger extolling his red mullet, mackerel, turbot, and swordfish.

Opposite Avellis' shop was a branch of the French post office, on the top floor of which a French dressmaker plied her trade and flirted with the Greek tailor and also with the Greek barber, both of whom had their establishments a few doors off. Nor must I forget the French book-shop, to which came the Perote lady to buy the latest French novels on the sly.

I follow Avellis upstairs into his old-fashioned, musty consulting-room, his sanctum—whither his patients of both sexes (veiled Turkish ladies with the rest) came to consult "Monsieur le Docteur"—with its mysterious bottles in which sundry medical viscera were preserved in spirits of wine, its cases of stuffed birds, and its aquarium. Two photographs of an Albanian peasant hung on the wall, one showing him deprived of his upper lip, the other with artificial nose and moustache supplied by Avellis by order of the Sultan, who subsequently took this man and many others into his service in the Palace after they had been mutilated by Christian Montenegrins in the great struggle of 1876.

When driving or walking through the city on a Sunday afternoon with Avellis, it used to surprise me to see the number of people who returned his greeting. Among them were some of the highest personages in the land, and their marked cordiality was in striking contrast to the treatment usually meted out in Europe to those of an inferior class.

Sauntering along the Grande Rue de Pera with him one Sunday afternoon, we were passed by a State carriage, drawn by two magnificent black horses, with that rich gilt harness peculiar to the Imperial family. It contained the present Sultan of Turkey, at that time, by force of circumstances, a do-nothing Prince under strict police and Palace spy surveillance, but by no means an indoor prisoner, as was currently reported. Avellis knew the Prince well, and gave me an interesting account of his sadness, his all-absorbing care and anxiety regarding the future of his country, his kind-hearted benevolence, and his unassuming simplicity of manner and character. Carried away by his admiration for the man, Avellis demonstratively took off his hat as the Prince drove past, who returned the unusual attention with evident satisfaction, though both actions were almost sure to have been noticed by spies and reported to the Palace: a proceeding which might well result in Avellis receiving a broad hint that a "Purveyor of Surgical Instruments to his Imperial Majesty the Sultan" must be more careful in future in the choosing of his friends.

It is true that all these people might have been brought into contact with Avellis through business; but it was not only business. "C'est un brave homme," say Turks and Rajahs alike. This in itself is sufficient to secure for a man the respect and goodwill of his fellow-citizens, even though he may not have five pounds in the world to call his own. And here it is only fair to mention that the Christian and Jewish population in Constantinople join with Mohammedans in paying respect to personal character. I have seen a crowd of hundreds of people—more than would be likely with us to be present at the funeral of many a man of worth and learning—follow one to his last resting-place, although during his lifetime all that could have been said of him was, "C'est un brave homme."

CHAPTER XII

THE TURK AND HIS CREED

Love thyself last: cherish those hearts that hate thee

Corruption wins not more than honesty.

Still in thy right hand carry gentle peace

To silence envious tongues. Be just, and fear not:

Let all the ends thou aim'st at be thy country's,

Thy God's, and truth's; then if thou fall'st....

Thou fall'st a blessed martyr.

SHAKESPEARE, *Henry VIII*

As I indite these pages, the rule of the Turk seems to be irrevocably destined to pass from Europe, not in consequence of his religious fanaticism, even less on account of his supposed cruelty, but owing to a feature of the Turkish character which is shared by other races whose instincts are in perpetual conflict with the modern surroundings of their existence. The North American Indian cannot be converted from habits engendered in the past. In a lesser degree the same may be said of the Celt in conflict with the Anglo-Saxon, and the Slav with the Teuton. In spite of a dominion of centuries in Europe, the Turk is still in his heart, and even in his habits, an Asiatic, and not only an Asiatic, but an Asiatic of a peculiar type—a born horseman with little aptitude for plodding, sedentary occupations, herein displaying marked divergence from the highly cultivated Chinese and Japanese.

In the most recent development of affairs in the Near East there is indeed something pathetic in the evident yearning of the Turk to turn towards his home—Asia. Instinctively his longing is directed towards the East, the resting-place where he may hope to be unmolested.

Professor Vambéry, writing to me under date November 12, 1912,[20] says: "The fate of our poor Turkish friends is sealed. They will get rid of the cumbersome European ballast, and it is to be wished that they should be able to recuperate in Asia, where they cannot be replaced by any other Moslem nation. Their collapse in Europe was inevitable, and it is only the suddenness of the fall which has surprised me."

20. See Appendix, p. 284.

But even if we accept the view that the Turk is by nature something of a nomad, and as such has never been much else than a stranger, an Asiatic in Europe, this should not deter us from recognizing the sterling human qualities which every unbiased foreigner who has visited the country must have observed as innate in the Turks as a people, and which mark the best of all classes.

And yet, with their minds centred on material aims, immersed in the humdrum conditions of life which this all-absorbing activity indicates, accustomed to subdue their feelings until many of them have lost the faculty of expressing, let alone giving way to, strong passion, how difficult it is for Europeans to form an idea, to realize what unrestrained human passions are like when they flare up in fierce hearts, and to make allowance for them. This must be more particularly the case when they are called into play by those traditional antagonisms of race to which many of the harrowing tragedies of the East are due; for other forms of crime, or rather instigations to crime, are probably fewer among the Turks than among Europeans. I was once a witness to a desperate encounter between some Montenegrins and Greeks in a German beer-house in Pera, and the memory of the diabolical fury of the Montenegrins is still present to my mind, together with the quiet self-control of the proprietor, an old Prussian soldier of '66 and of '70, who at last succeeded in calming the disputants. The passionate hatreds of the Near East are practically unknown to us.

With due reservation regarding these fierce outbursts, commonly, but in my humble opinion most unjustly, attributed to religious fanaticism, I am still of opinion that the Turk is far from being inclined by nature to cruelty. His kind treatment of animals, of horses and dogs, and of the birds in the air, which he takes no pleasure in shooting, speaks volumes for the humane attributes of the Turk, whose deep attachment to his own family and kindness to dependents nobody who knows the East can call into question. For instance, English governesses in Turkish families are treated with such consideration that they endeavour to avoid meeting their own countrymen and countrywomen, for fear that the difference in our treatment of dependents should expose them to humiliation in the eyes of their Turkish masters and mistresses.

As regards the accusation of fanaticism and intolerance so liberally levelled against the Turk, what are we to say to the incontrovertible fact that the Holy Sepulchre at Jerusalem has been under the protection of Turkish soldiers for centuries, and that no instance has ever been put on record of sacrilege or desecration at their hands, or could have been, since the Koran prescribes veneration for Christ and everything appertaining to our Saviour? How does this fit in by contrast with the record of rapine and destruction which all through the Reformation marked the struggles between Roman Catholics and Protestants, not only on the Continent of Europe, but also in England and Scotland, where, for instance, the ruins of the Cathedral of St. Andrews bespeak savage passions which are not extirpated even to-day from the hearts of many so-called Christians? Is it not a fact that only a few years ago, when the Eucharistic Congress was being held in London, the British Government could not see its way to allow the Host to be paraded through the streets of Westminster, whilst in Constantinople, on the day of Corpus Christi, the Host is borne through the streets escorted by Turkish Mohammedan soldiers? The dead of the Orthodox Greek Church are publicly exposed to view, a proceeding not allowed in Greece. Only a short time ago the dead body of their Archbishop, attired in his full robes, seated in his Archiepiscopal chair, was paraded through the streets and followed by a crowd of Greek prelates, accompanied and protected by Turkish soldiery. This happened whilst fierce war was raging between Greek and Turk, without a voice being raised by the Turks to deprecate a religious ceremony being held in public by enemies of their faith and country, and belonging to a creed which the Turks are supposed to loathe and detest.

The very words "The Terrible Turk," with their grim alliteration, seem to flow naturally from our tongue, without ever suggesting the thought that the Turk might be more than justified in applying the epithet to others. The Anglo-Saxon pesters him with his missionary activity, the Italian has robbed him of Tripoli, the Greek has annexed Crete and several islands, the latter-day German intrudes upon him with his noisy presence and his pestering commercial-traveller instincts, but above all the terrible Russian silently hovers ready to swoop on his country like some huge bird of prey.

The European, at least of the English-speaking world, who visits Constantinople for the first time usually arrives with extraordinary preconceptions regarding the mysterious ways, the cruelty and fanaticism of the Turk. If he be one of the open-minded few, a prolonged residence in Turkey will usually suffice to banish his previous opinions, to inspire him with sympathy, and to make him marvel how it could have been possible to harbour such false notions regarding a people and a country concerning which the average European knows so little. For there can be no doubt that our early training, the one-sided ideas of our youth due to clerical teaching from generation to generation, are the main causes of our conception of the Turks as cruel and depraved. Who of us has not been shocked as a boy in visiting the Chamber of Horrors at Madame Tussaud's and viewing the array of coloured prints depicting the horrible tortures said to have been inflicted upon dishonest traders in Turkey?[21] Well might Turkish Ambassadors have protested long ago against this method of prejudicing the English mind against Turkey, as Bismarck did in Paris, after the 1870 war, against the public exhibition of M. Edouard Détaille's well-known picture, "Nos Vainqueurs," which was removed in consequence. But the Turk is accustomed to suffer wrong in silence, and, as far as I know, has never complained officially.

> 21. As far as I recollect no explanation is vouchsafed with these drawings that they refer to the Turkey of the past. Hence the likelihood that many a cockney visiting Madame Tussauds goes away with the impression that they treat of Turkish practices of to-day.

The mystery attached to polygamy, our imaginary ideas concerning the position of Turkish women and the harem, may also have a great deal to do with our prejudice against the Turks.

We are taught in our youth to look upon the Crusades as expeditions undertaken to protect the Tomb of Christ from the desecrating hands of the Infidel. Serious historians are no longer under any delusion as to the political character of the Crusades. Thus if the Sacred Sepulchre was ever endangered by the Turks, how came it to pass that it was not destroyed long before the Christians ever reached Jerusalem? Is it not an historical fact that Jerusalem was in the possession of the Turks for centuries before the idea of protecting the Holy Sepulchre ever occurred to the Popes? If the Crusades were justified as undertaken for the protection of the Christians against the Turks, how came it to pass that so few Christians in the East ever joined the Crusades? From what we know of Christian fanatical intolerance, even down to comparatively recent periods, is it not rather more than likely, supposing the Holy Sepulchre had been situated in a Christian country, that its very site would long ago have been obliterated?

In the course of my various visits to Constantinople I used often to look up my kind friend Ahmed Midhat Effendi, and our many conversations, always fraught with instruction for me, embraced every imaginable subject. They turned especially upon the Mohammedan religion and the attitude of Christianity towards Islam, not merely in our time, but throughout past centuries. It needed no great powers of persuasion to convince me that the European frame of mind towards the Mohammedan world must needs be the outcome of a one-sided version of events. How could it be otherwise in view of the inaccessibility of the records of Mohammedan history? Thus Lessing's drama of "Nathan the Wise," and the portrayal of Sultan Saladin as the ideal type of chivalry and religious tolerance, struck the Western world at the time as a revelation. To-day no serious person who has given the slightest attention to the subject can doubt that, whatever may have been the policy of aggression of the great Moslem conquerors, the spirit of Islam was one of broad religious tolerance at a time when such a quality was practically non-existent in Europe. When Sultan Selim proposed to offer the Christian population of his dominions the alternative of embracing Islam or expatriation—or, if you will, extermination—it was the Sheikh ul Islam who appealed to the precepts of the Koran prescribing the duty of the Sultan to protect and safeguard his subjects, whatever their faith, which prevented Selim from carrying out his intention. It was thus owing in a large measure to the Koran that the Christian population in Asiatic and European Turkey was protected and enabled to prosper in days when no European public opinion could have possibly intervened on its behalf. While the Turk was thus practising religious tolerance Jews were burnt at the stake in Christian Spain; the most intelligent portion of the inhabitants of France, the Huguenots, were being persecuted for their faith and driven from their homes by Louis XIV, and in England the penalty of death awaited the priest who dared to say Mass.

These are weighty historical facts, without fully and constantly realizing which it is practically impossible for a Christian born and bred to be fair to the Mohammedan Turk, and approach the study of his customs and character in an impartial spirit.

Ahmed Midhat, in drawing my attention to a recent publication concerning the conduct towards Christians prescribed by the Koran for Mohammedans, wrote to me some years ago as follows:

"I do not know whether this document will be sufficient to bring home to you the calumny which the Christian world launches at us, in attributing to us a hatred for everything that is not Mohammedan, and more particularly for Christianity and Christians as such. But if you believe in my honesty, accept my assurance, tendered on my oath as a devout Mohammedan, on my honour as a gentleman, that such hatred has never existed among us....

"Quite recently I read Count de Castries' excellent book on the Islam faith.[22] De Castries is an old French officer who has lived many years in the Algerian deserts, and has become almost an Arab himself in language, habits, and even in religion. I call his book excellent not merely because it is favourable to us, but because it reveals the attitude of the Christian world towards Islamism. I recommend you strongly to read it. But before you do so, I would like to tell you that we Mohammedans have never produced a single poet or prophet in the East who has written against Christianity and Christians in the spirit of those thousand abominations in which the Italian, French, and Spanish troubadours sang of Islam. You will not find a single line in all our literature of the kind such as the hundreds cited by De Castries from Christian writers, and which justly arouse his indignation. I do not exaggerate, my dear friend, I merely tell you the naked truth. You can defy the Christian world to cite, not a single Mohammedan writer, but a single line in the whole of our popular literature which could inspire hatred of the Christian. Even the wars of the Crusades, which lasted through centuries, were powerless to change the sentiment of tolerance towards the Christian world, a sentiment for ever rooted in the spirit of the Koran—the Word of God revealed by His Hadis (the words of the Prophet) and by the legislation of His Imams the so-called Cheriat.

> 22. "L'Islam: Impressions et Études." Par le Comte Henri de Castries. Paris: Armand Colin.

"The hatred which the Christian world attributes so gratuitously to us is only the reflection of its own animosity towards us. The centuries which have elapsed since the Renaissance have been unable to efface this hatred from the spirit of Christianity. It is now half a century since Orientalists of different countries have been doing their best to eradicate these voluntary errors, and to spread the truth with regard to Islamism; but they have not been able to change the old Christian antagonism with regard to us. The last Græco-Turkish war fully demonstrated this. 'Cet animal est bien méchant. Quand on l'attaque il se défend!' Our legitimate defence against unprovoked aggression was accounted a crime because the aggressors were Christians and according to the words of the mediæval troubadours we are the 'Adorers of Moham.'

"I see that thoughtful minds, such as Father Hyacinthe, Draper, Carlyle, and others, are supposed to have investigated the tenets of Islamism. Is it really possible to make serious investigations into what you have been accustomed to look upon as a 'multitude of contradictory and false[23] conceptions—the barbarous ideas of a false Prophet, the sanguinary aspirations of a barbarian'?

> 23. That this outburst is not entirely unprovoked or unjustified seems to be proved by an extract from a public speech of the late Lord Salisbury, in which he spoke of England's antagonist in Egypt as representing "the most hideous side of barbarism which a false religion can produce"—this religion (the Mohammedan) being that of sixty millions of British subjects.

"And here I would say: The time for these blackguardisms, the fashion for these blasphemies, has passed. We live to-day in an age when everything has to submit to the process of analysis. We no longer rest satisfied with abstract ideas or despotic dicta. We insist upon the results of exact observation and study; we ask for concrete, logical judgment. You must study the Mohammedan faith; you must institute a fair, well-balanced comparison between our creed and other religions before you are in a position to judge, much less to condemn. Is such a comparison feasible? To my mind it is a task of supreme difficulty, and yet without an attempt in that direction it is impossible to be fair and unbiased towards the Mohammedan world."

An accusation against Islam which Midhat resented more than any other was its supposed antagonism to letters and learning, an accusation which, by the way, is sufficiently refuted by the history of the Moors in Spain. In this connexion Midhat used to cite the following words of the Koran: "Advance with your lances in order to make room for your pens"—the term for "lance" and "pen" being identical in Arabic. The Koran thus intended to convey the idea that warlike advance was only to make way for opportunities of culture and enlightenment.

Talking one day to Midhat on these and kindred matters, I said:

"Midhat, they tell me at a certain Embassy that you are a fanatical old Turk who hates the stranger within the gates; though, to be frank with you, if I were a Turk, I too should hate them with a vengeance, after all the uncharitable things they say about Turkey."

"And I tell you," replied Midhat, "that you have only to read up the unbiased records of our history to learn that tolerance is the very basis of our conduct. Does not the word of Mohammed tell us: 'Whosoever does wrong unto a Christian or a Jew shall find me as his accuser on the Day of Judgment'? Do not the Jews and the Mohammedans keep the same fasts and almost the same festivals? The principal difference I detect between them and us is that the Jews do not believe in Christ or Mohammed; whereas the Mohammedans believe in Moses, Christ, and the Prophets.

"The history of the Crusades (which has long since been, so to speak, a monopoly of the Christian world) is the greatest source of injustice to the Saracens. To-day it is acknowledged by those experts who have investigated this vast subject that the Christians domiciled in the East rarely made common cause with the Crusaders, and that those who did so were not molested by the Saracens after the withdrawal of the former. When the Crusaders of the Third Crusade got as far as Constantinople they found that the Byzantine Emperor and his Christian subjects were in close alliance with the Saracens. History relates that instead of directing their efforts against the Saracens, the Crusaders on more than one occasion fell out among themselves and robbed the Greeks. In fact, wherever the Crusaders went they brought rapine and seduction with them. Neither do we ever hear how it came to pass that the Christians in Asia never joined the Crusaders against the Saracens or assisted them in any way. Thus we are bound to assume that as far as their religion is concerned the Christian population was, at least at that time, not molested by the Mohammedans.

"I tell you that a Christian place of worship has never been desecrated by a Turk, except, as at the taking of Constantinople, during the heat of battle. And for this very simple reason: that the Koran expressly lays down that a Christian church is sacred as an edifice devoted to God, and must be respected as such. You yourself have had ample opportunity of seeing that this injunction has been strictly carried out in the past by the untouched condition of the many Christian monasteries on the road between Trebizond and Erzeroum. You can see it even in Constantinople to-day, where many mosques which were formerly Greek churches still show the images of Christian saints on the walls restored to-day, as they were over 500 years ago, notably in the Kaarie Mosque.[24] The fresco images of the saints of the Byzantine Church look down from the walls upon the Mohammedan worshippers.

> 24. Midhat Effendi himself took me over this particular mosque during one of my visits to Constantinople.

"As a matter of fact, it is wonderful to me how little differentiates the Moslem faith from the tenets of Christianity. It is true we do not accept the Trinity, but neither was it accepted as a dogma by the Evangelists; indeed, it is never once mentioned in the Old or New Testament. Also, at the Council of Nicæa (A.D. 325) only two hundred priests, backed by Constantine the Great, accepted this doctrine, but two thousand two hundred priests refused to subscribe to it.

"We Mohammedans accept Jesus as the Son of God. We also believe in the Holy Virgin. Indeed, in more than one respect the Mohammedans deviate little in their faith from the old Arian Christians of the period of Nestorius, Patriarch of Constantinople in the year 400 A.D. It is only within living memory that in self-defence Mohammedans have entered into a polemical contest with the Christian world. Even the notorious Lebanon troubles had little or nothing to do with religion and intolerance as such. They were almost entirely political in origin and character."

In a conversation which I had in November 1904 with Ahmed Midhat, he gave me the following explanation with regard to the creed of Islam:

"Je crois à un seul Dieu et ses anges et ses livres sacrés et ses Prophètes, et que le Bonheur et le Malheur viennent de lui. Jésus est parmi eux et qu'au dernier jour il sera là comme intercède auprès de Dieu. Nous ne demandons rien de Mahomet. Nous ne nous prosternons pas devant lui; il n'est pas notre idole. Il a besoin de nous. Nous prions Dieu pour son salut dans l'autre monde. Il est notre précepteur, notre Socrate. Pour devenir Mussulman il y a deux phrases qu'il faut citer et croire:

"(1) La ilahe illa Allah: Il n'y a Dieu que Dieu—Allah. Il n'est digne d'être adoré que Dieu.

"(2) Mohammadune ressoul Allah: Mahomet est son prophète."

Thus far Ahmed Midhat, who at least was[25] sincere, living as he preached, according to the laws of Mohammed. He was one of the living forces of the

Islamic world, whose name was known and honoured throughout Asiatic Turkey, as I had opportunity to convince myself in the fastnesses of Kurdistan, and have already related.

> <u>25</u>. Since this was first drafted I have been obliged to alter it into the past tense. For a letter I recently addressed to my friend comes back to me through the British Post Office at Constantinople, with the word "deceased" stamped upon it. When and how Ahmed Midhat passed away I know not; but were he alive I feel sure that the misfortunes of his beloved country would soon have broken his big but childlike heart.

Fortunately, the Christian world is not quite so blind to the human side of Mohammedanism as Midhat imagined. The late Sir Richard Burton—than whom no European possessed a keener insight into Oriental life—was once asked by a friend what creed he professed. He made the following reply: "I profess no creed; but if you ask me what I am, I would say more nearly Mohammedan than anything else. There is something sterling in that religion. The Mohammedans do what they profess, which is more than most Christians do." I for one believe that it is this sincerity which is the source of Turkish courage and Turkish dignity in misfortune.

Not only difference of religion, but the Oriental form of government explains the antagonistic attitude of the Western world towards Turkey and her Sovereign. As Khalif of Islam, the Sultan, according to Ahmed Midhat, comes in for the ill-will harboured unconsciously for centuries towards Islam by the Christian world. As an autocrat he also incurs the jealous displeasure of a rival Power—not the King of England nor the President of the United States, but the real governing despots of England and America—the easily excited passions of the masses; far more powerful, more prejudiced and intolerant than any ruling Sovereign in our time. This is indirectly proved by the fact that hatred of the Turk has manifested itself most passionately in those countries in which public opinion, with all its ignorance of other lands, ministered to by a sensational Press, is most powerful. Neither Scandinavia, Germany, Italy, nor France shares this bias to the same degree; and yet who would assert that they are not intelligent, educated communities imbued with high standards of conduct? For many years past these passions have been fed by those who have had an interest in fanning them into open flame. According to Napoleon I, a lie needs but twenty-four hours' start in order to become immortal. What are the chances of dispassionate truth when the start is one not of hours, but of generations?

The Turk may continue to deny officially this or that; but who reads with an open mind what he has to say for himself? Only those who have seen with their own eyes—such men as Burton, Gordon, Hobart, and the late Admiral

Commerell—have been fair-minded towards the Turk. The wealthiest men throughout the Turkish Empire are Greeks and Armenians; and yet we are asked to believe that these Christians, who probably own three-fourths of the real estate in the Turkish Empire, are sufferers under a grasping despotism!

On one occasion I was conversing with the chairman of the Ottoman Bank, Sir Edgar Vincent, who has since resigned and returned to England. He was tired of Constantinople. An Englishman of social tastes, he lacked congenial intercourse in Turkey. But one thing he told me he felt he should miss terribly in returning to Europe—the extraordinary freedom in Turkey! And as if by the irony of fate, it is this very liberty, this tolerance in Turkey which has powerfully contributed to the downfall of the Turk in Europe. For it is from Robert College, the Christian educational institution on the Bosphorus, which owes its very existence to the tolerance and benevolent munificence of successive Sultans that a number of Christian subjects of Turkey have gone forth into journalism and persistently blackened the character of the Turks and their ruler.

The following testimony to the spirit of Turkish tolerance was handed to me the last time I was at Constantinople by a distinguished fellow-countryman. I transcribe it here as it seems but natural that evidence from such a source should carry more weight than that of even the most unsophisticated Mohammedan:

"All religions are tolerated by the law of Turkey, and those who profess them are granted the fullest liberty to practise them. The only conditions exacted by the State are that each religious body must be duly authorized and that a responsible chief must be appointed, with whom the Government can treat in case of need.

"These spiritual heads enjoy several very remarkable privileges. They are ex-officio members of the Councils of the Provinces and Communes in which they live, and are thus enabled to protect the interests and rights, spiritual and temporal, of the members of the communion.

"The internal administration of all matters spiritual and temporal connected with their respective communities is entrusted by the Turkish law to the jurisdiction of the Patriarch, Grand Rabbi, Vekel, or Sheikh, as the case may be. They are also members of the Grand Council of the nation sitting at Constantinople, which regulates and prescribes the rights of the various communities.

"The communities recognized by the State, and which enjoy the privileges I have named as well as perfect liberty, are the following:

"1. Orthodox Turks, Orthodox Bulgarians, Armenians, Syrians, Jacobites, Copts, and Chaldean Nestorians.

"2. Rites in communion with Rome, viz. Latin Catholics, Uniate Armenians, Uniate or Melchite Greeks, Uniate Chaldeans, Uniate Syrians, Uniate Copts, Uniate Bulgarians and Maronites.

"3. Protestants of every description—Anglicans, Presbyterians, English and American Methodists, Baptists, etc.

"4. Four different types of Jews, five of Metoualis, and six of Druses.

"The Moslem finds it most difficult to understand and distinguish the difference between the to him amazing variety of sects all professing the Christian faith; this is one of the causes of the sterility of Christian missions in the East. The Turk lumps them together as *giaours* and regards them all with contemptuous indifference, wondering, indeed, why they did not remain in their own countries to convert each other, or at least to arrive at a common agreement as to what is the Christian faith before thrusting their antagonistic creeds upon the contented Moslem. Nevertheless, he is very tolerant of what he considers their eccentricities, and provides a guard at the Holy Sepulchre at Eastertide to prevent the Greek and Latin Christians from massacring one another for the love of God.

"In travelling through Palestine they are as free as in any of our Indian provinces. The laws may not be perfect—very few are—but they are found adequate in most cases to protect life and property. It is true that they were not always so. About a hundred years ago, and, indeed, until the middle of the nineteenth century, there was as little liberty in Turkey for the Christians as there is at the present day in Russia except for the Orthodox Greeks. But all that has long been changed in the Ottoman Empire. Seventy years ago Sultan Mahmoud thus publicly expressed himself:

"'I desire that in future a Moslem shall only be distinguished as such at his mosque, the Christian at his church, and the Jew at his synagogue.'

"In these words he manifested his intention to regenerate the Empire by the complete emancipation and assimilation of the races under his rule; he announced the inauguration of a new era of reform. But it was his son and successor, Abdul Medjid, who actually introduced the new system, the 'Tanzimat,' by the proclamation of the 'Hatti-Sherif of Gulhanè' on November 9, 1839. This was followed by the establishment of the Criminal Code in 1840 and the Commercial Code in 1850. Both of these were chiefly based upon the Code Napoléon and have worked well. But the most important enactment of all was the publication of the firman of 1854 which guaranteed the perfect equality of Christians and Moslems before the law. These were the first-fruits of the Sultan's efforts to carry into effect the reforms promised by the Hatti-Sherif of Gulhanè. The next stage of the Tanzimat was reached after the Crimean war by the Hatti-Humayoun of 1856, which extended the reforms to the civil and military administrations, etc." Thus far the authority I have quoted.

When we bear in mind the conservative nature of Orientals generally and their hatred of any departure from their national practices and traditions, it is truly wonderful that the changes brought about in the internal constitution of the Empire by these decrees have not resulted in a violent upheaval of the Moslem population. It is a remarkable proof of the respect and veneration in which the Sultan is held by his subjects that they should have submitted so peacefully to such a startling revolution in their national life.

It is most unlikely that any other nation would endure for a moment the encroachment on its status, the abuse of its hospitality, which the Turks have long submitted to at the hands of different European nations. No other nation would, in the long run, allow foreign newspaper correspondents to perpetrate the misrepresentations which have been indulged in for years past at Constantinople, unless, as in England, it felt it could afford to ignore calumny. One thing, however, is certain, that neither in France, Germany, Austria, nor Russia would the persistent campaign of misrepresentation which was carried on for years by foreigners enjoying the hospitality of the Turks, paying no taxes and in some cases making their fortunes in Turkey, be tolerated. All the above-mentioned countries can furnish cases in which foreign newspaper men have been summarily ordered to leave the country within a few hours for comparatively trivial offences. In the United States foreign journalists of such a type would probably find more serious consequences await them than mere banishment. No less noteworthy are the disgraceful facts connected with the promiscuous naturalization of Turkish subjects. Thus when I was in Constantinople in 1897, it was openly stated that the Greek Envoy, Prince Mavrocordato, in order to reward a man who carried his gun for him during a shooting expedition, made him a present of a Greek naturalization paper. The latter thus became a Greek subject, and as such entitled to all the immunities which foreigners have been entitled to under the well-known Capitulations, thanks to the easy-going tolerance of the Turks. The Armenians, being the most cunning of the Christian subjects of the Sultan, are the most successful in perpetrating these naturalization frauds, now and then with the connivance of foreign Powers.

In the course of my many visits to Constantinople I have repeatedly been made acquainted with instances of questionable newspaper correspondents who came up to the Palace with the scarcely veiled intimation that it was to be a case of pay or slander. During the Armenian disturbances in 1896 a French female journalist went up to the Palace and openly declared that she intended to be paid or to write up "atrocities."

Such are a few of the influences which have been at work to cause trouble in the Turkish Empire, and such the basis upon which is founded the most hypocritical agitation known the world over, that of the Russians in favour of their Christian "brethren" in Turkey. Who that has visited Russia as well as Turkey, and has a spark of fairness left in his composition, would not cry out in indignation at the hypocrisy of it?

No wonder Turks are loth to become reconciled to a state of things which none but this ever-patient race would have put up with so long, and have turned for sympathy to others who, whatever their selfish motives, have been less tainted with these intrigues against the laws of hospitality and common decency.

CHAPTER XIII

TURKISH TRAITS

A jewel in a ten-times-barred-up chest

Is a bold spirit in a loyal breast.

Shakespeare

THERE would seem to be two distinct strains of character influencing principle and conduct in the Turks. The one is that of the Turanian, the conquering Asiatic as typified, even before the Christian era, in a Mithridates, and subsequently in Attila, Tamerlane, Timur, Ghingiz Khan. The other is that of the Arab, whose code of life is contained in the teaching of Islam, with its gospel of placability and charity. Sultan Selim I represented the one in causing 40,000 Schiites to be exterminated. It is related that when he proposed to convert by force or exterminate the Christian population of his dominions, he was opposed, as already mentioned, by the Arab element in the person of the Sheikh ul Islam, who exhorted him to remember that Mohammed inculcated the duty of protecting, not harming, the Christians. These antagonistic currents were blended most harmoniously in the person of the renowned Saladin of Crusading fame. Down to the present day the Turks have instinctively recognized this duality and accepted it in the person of the Sultan, whilst they themselves have adhered to the teaching of Mohammed and by it regulated their own conduct. This explains why the Turkish people view the irresponsible acts, the extravagances, and the severities of their rulers so leniently as rightly appertaining to their exalted position; whereas the Turk himself is remarkably free from such tendencies. It explains their appreciation of the hard-working, industrious qualities of their Sultan as these were typified in Abdul Hamid, and their contempt for a lazy Sovereign like Abdul Aziz, though they themselves as a people rather incline to the indolence of a tranquil and contemplative life. Only when roused beyond endurance, excited and perplexed, is the Turk galvanized into quick action and apt to be resentful and cruel. Great crises find him placid and calm. The vast mass of the Mohammedan people is deeply imbued with its own code of ethics, and carries it into practice with a single-minded sincerity to which it would be difficult to find a parallel. From this point of view the Turk may be considered not so much "worldly" as "other-worldly."

A deal of the mental acumen which with us is directed towards business and the accumulation of wealth is devoted in the case of the Turks to other and higher objects. While wealth and worldly position are our aims, and failure to achieve either spells life bankruptcy, the Turk appreciates conduct and good deeds as expounded in the Koran above everything else. According to Guglielmo Ferrero, "the Moslem can never pardon the unlimited materialism of Europeans." Right conduct in all the situations of life is impressed upon him by the law of Mohammed, and in this respect the Moslem is more removed from European thought than in any other, inasmuch as there is a harmony between his precepts and his practice. He sees the stranger bowing down to rank and worldly position, whereas with him class distinctions are scarcely more than official. In Turkey, outside a comparatively few wealthy families—many of which are Phanariote Greek Christians who have supplied high official servants for generations to the Turkish State, and hold themselves somewhat aloof from the Mohammedans—there is little superiority of caste or the arrogance of class consciousness. The current standards are, in conformity with the teaching of the Koran and the New Testament, humanely democratic. Ahmed Midhat was at one time talked of as a possible Grand Vizier, for the Sultan was convinced of his integrity as well as of his ability. The fact that his father was a seller of cloth, or that he himself began life as an apprentice, was so far from constituting any disadvantage that neither he nor his friends would have been able to understand the idea of his humble parentage being in any way derogatory. All the less so since he was a man of magnificent presence, one of the comparatively few in Constantinople who by their appearance recalled the Sultans of the zenith of Ottoman power, who were fathers at sixteen and still added to their family at the age of seventy. So little does obscurity of birth constitute a stigma that a Turk, after having once been a servant who took charge of the goloshes of visitors left outside on entering a Turkish private house, became a pasha and was given the name of Papoudji (or slipper) Pasha; this cognomen was accepted by him and his friends rather as a compliment than otherwise. A Turk would be despised who was ashamed of, or endeavoured to hide, his humble antecedents, or denied his poor relations. He has no understanding of those who, having got on in the world, neglect or cut themselves adrift from their connexions because these have become irksome and they are ashamed of them. When a man rises to high position in Turkey he remembers only too readily those who belong to him, and now and then gets himself into trouble by helping his poor relations or those who have been friends of his obscure youth; and this often without any other motive than the satisfaction to be derived from a kind action. For in Turkey high position is supposed to be a reward for zeal in service, for conduct, and is freely open to all classes. That it is often bestowed upon the unworthy is only to say that judgment and selection are fallible in Turkey as elsewhere; but there can be no doubt that service rendered is in the first instance the test.

It is only among the Turks who have mixed with Europeans, particularly in diplomacy, that you find that hauteur, that "class-selfish arrogance," and that degree of cynicism which have been acquired in social intercourse in the capitals of Europe. From the ranks of these Europeanized Turks sprang the artificial element who upset the ancient régime, with small prospect, as we now see, of putting anything better in its place.

But if obscurity of origin does not constitute a bar to advancement it would be a mistake to suppose that the Turks attach no weight to an illustrious ancestry. Izzet Pasha introduced me, as already mentioned, to a Ulema at the Palace who, he assured me, could trace his descent not only from Mohammed, but back to Abraham. Their conception of an aristocracy is one of descent from men renowned for their virtues.

So great is the value which the Turks attach to conduct that, even in their favourite authors, they do not rest satisfied with precept or with doctrine, but look, besides, for conduct. Thus those of philosophic bent are not attracted by Voltaire or even by Schopenhauer. They are influenced by such thinkers as Büchner, Justus Möser, Spinoza, and Herbert Spencer, who lived as they taught. Conduct is verily the keystone of Mohammedan ethics, for while the Sultan is accepted as the direct representative of Mohammed in the eye of the Faithful, the Sheikh ul Islam, although in a sense himself a nominee of the Sultan, possesses final authority as interpreter of the word of the Prophet. He is invested with far more real authority than that possessed by any priest in the world with the single exception of the Pope of Rome. The Sheikh ul Islam may be said to be the spiritual watchman set by Mohammed to control the conduct of his worldly successors. The most ominous feature, as I was repeatedly assured in connexion with the later years and tragic end of Sultan Abdul Aziz, was that he had incurred the censure of the Sheikh ul Islam and through this had lost caste with the Sheikhs, Mollahs, and Ulemas, and lastly had aroused the hostility of the Softas. They accused him of neglecting his duties and leading a life of idleness. Months before his dethronement the mosques of Constantinople were deserted even on days of high festival.

Whatever some Turks may think of the form of government under which they live, and more particularly of the centralization of power in the hands of a Sultan, their appreciation of Abdul Hamid as a man could be gauged by anybody who had the opportunity of mixing freely with them. Most illuminating were casual comments, inasmuch as they often reflected the ideals of the people. The Turk never talks for the sake of talking, and scorns the rhetorical tricks of the actor. He is a sincere and a dignified man. You never heard the Sultan extolled as a great sportsman or a war lord, rarely as a statesman, although Abdul Hamid enjoyed a high and probably an exaggerated reputation in this respect. But you would often hear him praised as being good and kind. "Sa Majesté est si bon; il est un vrai gentilhomme," and above all, "C'est un Sultan travailleur," "Il travaille jour et nuit pour le bonheur de son peuple, ses sujets," were expressions I often heard in private conversation.

If a visitor felt that he had been slighted where he deemed he was entitled to some attention on the part of the Sultan, the Turks would apologize for their ruler and tell the stranger that he must not be harsh in his judgment, as His Majesty was busy day and night working for the good of his vast dominions. More than this, the Sultan was not above apologizing himself to quite minor folks if they had done him good service and he fancied that he had failed in attention towards them. "Tell Mr. X I have been so busy with one thing and another that I have not been able to see him and thank him as he deserves for the services he has rendered our country." This was by no means an unusual message for a stranger to receive from the Sultan. Indeed, it is a question whether the Sultan did not owe his popularity rather to his being a true representative of some of the most marked Turkish traits of character, such as a sense of gratitude, generosity, simple distinction, and hospitality, than to his political abilities as a ruler.

It has been asserted that the sentiment of democratic brotherhood and disregard for the privileges of birth and caste are responsible for the downfall of the Turkish régime. I am inclined to think that it has been largely the human attributes indicated above which enabled an anachronistic system of uncontrolled autocracy to live so long.

Nobody knew the Turkish character more thoroughly than my good friend Avellis. Never have I met a more enthusiastic champion of their virtues or a more earnest apologist for their defects.

"Believe me," Avellis would say, "if you find a Turk is dishonest, you may be sure that he belongs to the gang of pashas at the Palace, or that he has imbibed roguery from contact with Levantine Christians or Europeans. A long residence in European capitals deprives him of his most sterling and attractive characteristics. It robs him of his faith and his unspoilt patriarchal virtues, with their intensely human attributes. When he loses his faith he acquires in its place the sceptical cynicism which distinguishes the upper classes in every European capital." Avellis believed that European society had a debasing influence on the Turk, just as the European on coming to Constantinople, unless of an exceptionally fine type, becomes vitiated by associating with the Levantine. "There is no finer man on earth than the uncontaminated Turk. I have often signed contracts with Turks without understanding their contents (for I read their writing with difficulty)," continued Avellis, "and I would not hesitate to do so again. I know them to be incapable of falsehood or deception, unless debased by intercourse with Europeans. The unspoilt Turk is incapable of dishonesty. No one practises the virtues of humanity, the tenets of faith and charity to such a degree as he.

Be a Turk ever so poor, no beggar will appeal to his hospitality in vain. Let us suppose it is the end of the Ramadan Fast. He is just sitting down to his first frugal meal after the prescribed fast, and one still poorer than he enters and solicits a morsel of food. As often as not he will exclaim: 'Boujourun Effendem,' meaning 'Welcome, sir, help yourself.' If there is not enough for two he may even invite the stranger to partake of what he himself was about to eat, too proud to let his guest think that he had not already satisfied his own hunger.

"You must know the best type of Turk intimately to realize the extent of his generosity, of his sense of gratitude, the delight he takes in giving pleasure to others—that true test of love of our fellow-men. Then note his freedom from envy, the petty jealousies, trickeries, and arrogance which are such unlovable traits of my own countrymen, the Germans, whose overbearing demeanour of late years has become more and more objectionable in Turkey.

"Think of the patience and forbearance of the Turks in tolerating abuses of the liberty granted to aliens. No Government in any other country of the world would put up with the like of it. The Greeks are the most unabashed offenders. They parade their dead through the streets of Constantinople with the face of the corpse exposed, a morbid exhibition which is not allowed in Greece. Look at the disgraceful orgies of disorder among the Greek colony of Constantinople on the celebration of the Orthodox Greek Easter Day, with men discharging firearms promiscuously in the street from Saturday evening till Monday morning. Every year a number of people are wounded, if not killed, by accidents on these occasions."[26]

> 26. During my last visit to Constantinople—it was at Easter-time—I was invited to the house of a Levantine pasha, but the dinner had to be put off because his Greek cook had injured his hand by firing off a rusty old pistol in celebration of Easter Day.

During my various visits to Turkey I have had ample opportunities of hearing the opinions held by those who have mixed with the best Turks with respect to them. No testimony is more valuable than that of cultured Englishmen who have lived long in the East, more particularly such as have been engaged in a large way in commerce, or held positions in the Turkish naval and military service. In this connexion I may mention the well-known English family of merchant princes of which at that time the late Sir William Whittall was the head. The very name of Whittall has long been a passport throughout Asiatic Turkey, guaranteeing safe conduct in remote regions where scarcely a European is seen for years and years together. Such Englishmen are thorough-going admirers of the Turkish character and are distinct from those who have done so much by journalistic work to estrange England from Turkey, and Turkey from England.

Many are the stories told of the simple-minded attachment of the Turks to their employers, their superiors, even though these be Christians, and thus presumably with little affinity with them. Prince Alexander of Battenberg could not speak too highly of the fidelity of the Mohammedan element among his Bulgarian subjects: their orderliness, their freedom from crime, their childlike loyalty to him. After an important debate in the Sobranje—the Bulgarian Parliament—the Mohammedan members would call upon him privately at the Palace of an evening and seek instructions from him how he wished them to vote.

My old friend, Admiral Sir Henry Woods Pasha, who has been more than thirty years in the Turkish service, could never tell me enough of the devotion of the Turkish sailors under his command. Count Szechenyi Pasha, the Hungarian nobleman who for many years was at the head of the Constantinople Fire Brigade, which he originally organized, after having learned the business as an apprentice under the late Captain Shaw in London, is another of those who hold a high opinion of the fidelity and devotion of the Turks. Such evidence from men in whom the gentleman was innate before they had been lifted into rank and position by the Sultan is most valuable. They were inspired with gratitude towards their benefactor and declined to turn against him in the hour of his difficulties. One who had been approached with this object in view during the Armenian crisis indignantly replied: "No, I cannot, I will not bite the hand that has fed me." Alas, that there were too few of this stamp among the men Abdul Hamid distinguished by his favour.

There is probably no city, Moscow not excepted, in which so many fires take place as in Constantinople. The flimsy woodwork of the houses in the Turkish quarters, which the heat of a Constantinople sun turns in course of time to tinder, partly accounts for it. Nor must the temptation to arson among the Greeks and Armenian trading element be lost sight of. Most of the insurance is done in English offices, for the English insurance offices have hitherto been those which have met claims most handsomely and with fewest awkward questions. I have repeatedly watched the firemen as, with bare legs and chests, they rushed breathless in a body in the wake of the fire-engine across the Galata Bridge to some fire in the Stamboul quarter. One could not help being impressed by their evident whole-hearted enthusiasm, though they got little pay and no reward, and it was easy to understand how in times gone by a rush of half-naked Turkish warriors, sword in hand, has proved well-nigh irresistible against clumsily moving knights in armour and awkward pikemen. This might even explain victorious inroads up to the very walls of Vienna. The development of modern firearms and tactics, for which the Turk by his temperament is ill-fitted, seems to account for the modern defeats of the Turks far more than any racial decline. Where the virtues of courage, sincerity, piety, and self-sacrifice have admittedly remained unchanged, it would be absurd to talk of degeneration. What can be admitted is that the character of this fine race may be no longer fitted to cope successfully with the intricate demands of a modern, highly systematized civilization.

CHAPTER XIV

TURKISH TRAITS: II

Poor honest lord, brought low by his own heart,

Undone by goodness! Strange, unusual blood,

When man's worst sin is, he does too much good.

SHAKESPEARE, *Timon of Athens*

THE conditions of life under an autocracy naturally tend towards a sense of loyalty degenerating into adulation and servility on the part of public servants, as well as towards greed and corruption on the part of those whose high position places endless opportunities for dishonesty within their reach.

To estimate the character of the Turk, therefore, by the corruption at the Palace would not be fair to him. As well might we ourselves be judged by the wiles of the company promoter or the outside broker in the City of London. For despotism, however well intentioned, offers a similar field of operations for the dishonest; only the thousands who are annually robbed and ruined in the City of London, and the doings of the vultures who rob them, are not nearly so much in the public eye as the rogueries of the influential parasites in Turkey.

Strange it is that side by side with despotic authority and its narrowing effect on the development of character there should still exist an extraordinary appreciation of personal worth, intellectual and moral. You will never hear a Turk refer to a man as being rich, or as being "worth so much." All the time I spent among them I never once knew a Turk single out such qualifications as worthy of remark. A man's value lies in his character. Thus he is "instruit, fidèle, un homme qui a rendu de grands services et en rendra encore." Neghib Bey, a dark-eyed Syrian, exclaims: "Speak not to me of politicians, nor of men of wealth. I am ready to make use of them, but they do not otherwise attract me. Rather let me meet those of high thought, of talent, of genius, men with ideals. To obtain such as friends and to resemble them would be my ambition."

The greatest stress is laid upon the fidelity of those who have shown themselves to be true. When a deserving person received a reward a common remark would be: "Yes, he has received a favour of His Majesty, but he well deserves it." Instead of being envious when he sees a friend distinguished above him, the Turk rejoices in the exaltation of that friend. It has come under my notice more than once that when somebody received a distinction from the Sultan his friends were pleased, and said even exultingly to him: "You will obtain yet higher recognition, because you deserve it (parce que vous l'avez mérité)." It is ever a recurring reference to what you have done and for which you should be richly rewarded.

Great is the gratitude of the Turk for sympathy shown to him. Partisanship he does not look for. The most that he hopes for is freedom from prejudice and fairness towards his race and his religion. Should the stranger go so far as to betray a partiality for his country, a liking free from the suspicion of its being quickened by an expectation of baksheesh, his satisfaction is as genuine as it is spontaneous. A Frenchman is astonished if the stranger does not admire everything French; the Englishman is apt to be disdainful if the foreigner does not immediately admit the superiority of everything English. The Turk is more modest and self-restrained, and he is thankful if his feelings are not hurt by the "Frank."

His appreciation is apt to show itself in the smallest matters. One day, as I was about to go to the bazaar to buy a present, Ahmed Midhat offered to let one of his uniformed officials accompany me. This, said he, would ensure my being treated fairly by the Mohammedan traders. On going round that part of the bazaar known as "Bezestan," mostly tenanted by Mohammedans, I stopped before a stall belonging to a magnificent type of Turk. He might have been an Assyrian king as far as appearance and dignity of manner went. He sat, with legs crossed, perched up on high, immediately behind his show-case of curios—old watches and silver and gold bric-à-brac of all sorts. I pointed to a riding whip made of rhinoceros horn, mounted in gold, and asked the price. The answer my companion got was, "Tell your friend that it is the work of the Frank" (European workmanship), implying thereby inferiority in quality. He had been informed by the official accompanying me that, as I was a friend of the Osmanli, he was to treat me as one of themselves. Thus he did not want me to purchase an inferior article, even though he would have made a profit by selling it to me.

The Turk holds in grateful memory the names of those foreigners who have rendered Turkey unselfish service, even though it be generations ago. Of Englishmen, Hobart Pasha is still remembered; of Germans, Moltke. More remarkable still, a Vienna doctor, Professor Riedler, who organized the School of Medicine at Constantinople as far back as the reign of Sultan Mahmoud, more than eighty years ago, is to this day held in honour by the Turks, and this in an age of kaleidoscopic changes and short memories!

The genuine spirit of hospitality of the Turks, the noble traditions of which have come down to us through the Arabs, together with their chivalry, has long been recognized, in spite of the fanaticism of Christian detractors. The lavish hospitality to be found in Spain is perhaps traceable to a common

Arabian origin; for it is significantly absent as a distinctive trait among all the other branches of the so-called Latin races. Its most remarkable feature is the custom, when a visitor expresses admiration for an object belonging to his host, of immediately offering it to him. This still obtains in Spain, and is to be met with, as I have myself experienced, in distant Kurdistan.

But it is not among those who have gold and silver to dispose of that Turkish hospitality or other Turkish qualities can be tested. What really constitutes the most interesting feature of Turkish character is that these virtues are to be seen practised among the humblest classes. Thus, whereas Emerson's renowned treatise on "English Traits" deals almost exclusively with types of character observed among the well-born, no study of Turkish character could be complete, or, in fact, of any value, which did not deal with the characteristics which are to be found throughout the broad strata of the Mussulman population. Writers of Emerson's spirit deal with the apex of a pyramid; he who deals with the Turks must treat of its broad base—the great mass of the Turkish population, which alone adequately reflects the many excellent qualities of the Mohammedan world.

There is ample evidence that the Turks in their prime, notably when they became the conquerors of Constantinople and overthrew the corrupt Byzantine Empire, felt contempt for the Christians they came across. Thus, when the arrival of the Ambassador of the Holy Roman Empire was signalled at the Sublime Porte, the answer came, "Let the *giaour* be admitted"; and when, after his audience, the illustrious person was dismissed by the Grand Vizier, it might even happen that he would be pelted with eggs by the crowd. But there was more of good-natured contempt than of animosity in this treatment. Of intolerance to the Christian faith there was none at this period. Not only the Christian but the Jewish population lived free and unmolested in Constantinople.

The tolerance which the Jews have always enjoyed in Turkey is well known. At the time when they were being burnt at the stake in the public square in the town of Valladolid in Spain, Jewish overseers were deputed by the Jewish community in Constantinople to sit in the public bakehouses and see that the bread which was baked for Jewish consumption was prepared according to Jewish rites. Individual Jews were even permitted by the authorities to exercise a kind of police supervision over the Turks themselves at a time when their co-religionists were being exterminated like vermin in some Christian countries. Under Sultan Suleyman, one of the most influential of Turkish Ministers of Foreign Affairs was a Christian, Ludovico Gritti, a son of Andrea Gritti, the Doge of Venice. Sultan Suleyman even went so far as to have his portrait painted by a Christian, Melchior Lorenz, an inhabitant of Flensburg. One of the men most honoured by Sultan Mohammed Fatè, the conqueror of Constantinople, was again a Christian, an Italian of the name of Gentil Gellini, who was treated by the Turkish monarch with the greatest distinction. When subsequently war broke out between Venice and Turkey, the Sultan commissioned Gellini to take back to Venice the body of Enrico Dandolo, a former Doge, the first conqueror of Constantinople, during the Fourth Crusade, whose sarcophagus was found in the Church of Saint Sophia. Even the outbreak of war and all the supposed fanaticism of the Turks did not prevent a Turkish Sultan from pursuing a course of conduct which, even after five centuries, would be looked upon as an exceptionally chivalrous action among Christians.

When I was in Salonica there was no virulent Turkish Press to hound on the Turks against the Greeks, although a large proportion of the inhabitants in Salonica, albeit Turkish subjects, were Greeks in open sympathy with the Greek cause, even joining Greek committees, an act of high treason—in every country but Turkey. Nor did the Greeks take any trouble to hide this feeling, poring over the Greek newspapers in public as they arrived day by day. Yet no signs of popular resentment were visible during my stay on the part either of the populace or of the soldiery. The same passive toleration was to be observed in Constantinople, where the narrow streets leading to the French Consulate in Pera were crowded with Greeks seeking to obtain the protection of the French Embassy. They were not molested in any way. This might, perhaps, seem to be a matter of course, if we were not reminded of what happened to the Germans in Paris at the outbreak of the war in 1870.

How little is known of the record of the Turks in offering shelter to the oppressed of other races! Who was it that sheltered the Hungarian revolutionists who, when captured, were hanged or imprisoned? Is it not an historical fact established beyond question that a Sultan of Turkey risked war with Austria and Russia combined rather than break the sacred laws of hospitality of Mohammed, and surrender the Hungarian leaders Kossuth, Görgey, and many others? How do these facts, I ask, tally with the slander heaped upon the Turkish people and their rulers?

In no country in Europe are there so many foreigners, both as regards nationality and religion, as in Turkey, and nowhere else would aliens have a chance of such careers as some of them have made there. And yet I never came across any signs of Turkish jealousy. I have heard Turks speak with the highest respect of individual foreigners whom the Sultan had loaded with favours, but who at least had shown gratitude and attachment to the interests of their adopted country. We have only to think of the Dutch crew of adventurers who came over with William III from Holland to find an analogy, and compare the sentiments of the English towards them with those of the Turks towards foreigners in high place and pay in Turkey to illustrate even more closely the generosity of the Turks, and how far they can go in their tolerance of an alien element. Such favouring of the foreigner, even if it could exist in other countries, would inevitably evoke intense jealousy and intrigue on the part of the natives.

Speaking of a foreign pasha noted for his bumptious arrogance, and referring to some of his countrymen, a high-placed Turk said to me: "Que voulez-vous, mon cher? On les tolère." But whatever the Turks may feel, they have never shown it by malevolence towards foreigners who were in the employ of their Government.

Many Turkish Ambassadors abroad have at different times been Christians. The Turkish Ambassador in Berlin some years ago was a Greek, who, mainly through his position as Ambassador, was enabled to make a rich marriage. Far from feeling any gratitude to the Turkish Government for his career, he left his private fortune to some Greek institution at Athens, although at that particular moment Greece was meditating war against Turkey.

We have had of late years only too many instances of Christian ministers lending themselves to denunciation and depreciation of the Moslem. I have gleaned from the lips of missionaries, and their wives more rabid than themselves, both in Macedonia and in Asia, how ignorant prejudice can blind the understanding. A pathetic instance of this, verging on imbecility, is to be found in a book written by an Englishwoman which circulates in the Tauchnitz Collection of British authors, entitled "Diary of an Idle Woman in Constantinople."[27] In relating that she had seen a eunuch at the Selamlik with the Sultan's ladies, she exclaims: "He was a fat giant, a wretch." Why a poor devil who has been deprived of manhood should be a "wretch" the ingenuous authoress does not explain. Yet, so far as my experience goes, a good deal of what has been written in disparagement of the Turks has no better logical foundation than this exclamation. For all that, there can be no doubt that this eunuch abomination is a feature of Turkish life which has always created a strong prejudice in the Christian world against the Mohammedans. Hence it is not without interest to emphasize once for all that this unnatural institution is not of Mohammedan origin at all, but, as well as every other kind of human mutilation, is strictly forbidden by the Koran. Eunuchs were a common feature in antiquity, and in spite of the efforts of both Constantine the Great and the Emperor Justinian to do away with them they were quite common among the "good" Christians of the Byzantine Empire. Even at the present day the eunuchs in Constantinople—who, by the way, are only to be found in the household of the Sultan and of a few wealthy pashas—are supplied from the Christian monasteries of the East, notably those of Abyssinia.

27. Vol. 2921, p. 320.

Is it to be wondered at that people nurtured on misleading data can scarcely be brought to believe that there is less crime in Turkey than in almost any other country; that the punishment for crime is far more lenient than in most countries; that the deposed Sultan was never known to sign a death-warrant; and that the Mohammedan Turks, as distinct from the Christian inhabitants of the Levant, are so kind to animals of every variety, beast or bird, that a Society for the Protection of Animals, however vigilant, would find its occupation gone in Turkey?

The Turk's kindness to the dogs of the capital, since exterminated, is well known, as is also his kind treatment of horses. The beneficent results of this can be witnessed by the visitor to Constantinople when he sees saddled horses standing, free and unfettered, for hours by the kerbstone waiting to be hired, as docile as dogs, without anybody looking after or controlling them.

One of the favourite sports of the Christian Levantine population in Turkey is to shoot all kinds of singing birds, which are served up in restaurants in the Turkish national dish, pilaf. Any day in the autumn one can see crowds of doughty Christian Nimrods, armed with guns, going out in quest of the lark and the throstle, but never a Mohammedan Turk. This sight is a disgusting one to all lovers of nature, and when I was last in Constantinople the wife of the German Ambassador availed herself of the opportunity of an audience with the Sultan to intercede for the little songsters, asking His Majesty to issue an Iradè that they should not be exterminated.

If procrastination and dilatory methods of business are sometimes calculated to bring a highly strung European or American to despair in Turkey, patience and forbearance and long-suffering, on the other hand, rise with the Turks to the dignity of virtues. Rarely are these virtues more striking than in connexion with the calumny to which the Turk is continually subjected. Mehmet Izzet said to me, in the midst of a storm of invective let loose by the English Press upon the Turks: "Mon cher, nous sommes un peuple taciturne, nous ne pouvons pas nous défendre."

One day I was present at the Palace when an elderly man was engaged in earnest conversation with Izzet Pasha, the Second Secretary of the Sultan, supposed to be the most influential, as well as the most unscrupulous, man in Turkey. As the conversation was in Turkish I could not follow it, but the tone of supplication of the visitor was so marked that it made me think it must be a question of imploring mercy for some serious delinquency. So I ventured to say: "My dear Pasha, I hope you will be merciful to that poor fellow." "Mon cher," he replied, "the fact of the matter is that he is Governor of Jerusalem, and he wants me to get him a better appointment. We are old school-fellows, and I would like to oblige him, but it is quite beyond my power to do so in this instance."

Ample contact with the Turks in all manner of positions in life has convinced me that many of the wicked stories circulated about them have no better foundation in fact than the supposition involved in the above incident, of which I was an eye-witness.

Those who are acquainted with the character of Turkish women cannot speak too highly of their kindness of heart and their devotion to their children. During the Armenian massacres there were many instances of Armenians who sought refuge in the harem, and were saved by the interposition of Turkish women. This is all the more noteworthy since in other countries, notably those of Latin race, in times of great political excitement the women—as was the case with the Paris Commune in 1871—are often far more ferocious than the men. But here, among the Mohammedan women, mercy was to be met with—

No ceremony that to great ones 'longs,

Not the king's crown, nor the deputed sword,

The marshal's truncheon, nor the judge's robe,

Become them with one-half so good a grace

As mercy does.[28]

    28. Shakespeare: "Measure for Measure," II. 2.

The stranger, whatever his opportunities, only comes into contact with one-half of the Mohammedan population; the other is barred from his observation, from his very sight. In the course of all my visits to Turkey I never had an opportunity of approaching a Turkish woman within speaking distance. Even when I visited Ahmed Midhat, at his patriarchal residence at Beikos on the Bosphorus, in spite of our intimacy I saw no woman, though it was a large family gathering.

Avellis was my principal source of information regarding Turkish women, as he now and again was admitted to the harem in connexion with his calling. He often spoke to me of the distinction and the kindliness of the Turkish lady. But their graceful bearing was easily observable as they alighted from their carriages to shop in the Grande Rue de Pera. Their costumes—the quality of the rich silks of dark hues of blue or purple—were all noticeable, and indicative of good taste. Never have I seen a gaudily attired Turkish lady.

Only once was I privileged to obtain an idea of the impulsive kindness of their hearts. It was one afternoon at Scutari, when I went with Avellis and two ladies to visit the English cemetery. A closed carriage passed us, which, to judge by the richly gilt harness and the striking uniform of the menservants, evidently belonged to some high-placed Turk. Not until the third time it passed us did it attract our attention, when our two ladies had separated from us and had gone a little ahead. Then we saw all on a sudden two veiled faces lean out of the carriage and kiss their hands to the beautiful English-woman with auburn hair and angel face. Never am I likely to forget this incident, since she who was thus distinguished by high-bred Turkish ladies was the mother of my children.

A feeling of clannish affection for their family is said to be especially strong among Turkish women. It shows itself in their lasting attachment to their family long after they have left their homes and been separated from their kith and kin. For many of the women of the Imperial harem and of those of the great dignitaries of State come from the interior of Asia Minor, and are of lowly origin. Yet they keep up a regular communication with their relations in distant parts of the Empire, and are often the means of bringing these relations to Constantinople, where they are now and then given good appointments. Hassan Bey, the Circassian who assassinated Hussein Avni Pasha, the Minister of War, in open Council (June 15, 1876), was a brother of the favourite mistress of Sultan Abdul Aziz, whose death he wanted to avenge.

A certain primitive simplicity in the Mohammedan character—not the least of its attractions—is pointedly illustrated by the following incidents drawn from Mohammed's life, for which, as for so much else in these pages, I am indebted to my deceased friend Ahmed Midhat.

In his early days Mohammed belonged to a humble sphere of life. At the age of twenty-four he married the widow of a rich merchant in whose employ he had been in a subordinate capacity. He remained devotedly attached to her, although she was sixteen years his senior. Only after her death did he marry again; but his thoughts would still revert to the one he had lost and to whom he owed his rise in the world. This excited the jealousy of his second wife, with whom otherwise he lived most happily. One day she pressed him to assure her that she was as dear to him as his first wife had been. "I love you dearly," Mohammed replied, "but do not ask me to say that I love you as much as Chadidja, for she was the first human being to believe in me." It was only after his first wife's death that Mohammed, at the age of forty, really came forward and proclaimed himself a leader of men with a divine mission.

It is related of Mohammed that when he felt his end approaching he summoned his followers around him, and, being still possessed of sufficient strength to address them, told them that he knew his days were numbered, and he wished to ask whether there was anyone present who could say that he had done him a wrong; if so, he was ready to crave his forgiveness. They replied with one voice that Mohammed had been their friend and benefactor and that he had wronged no man. Then someone got up and said he had a claim against him. On a certain occasion he had been present when a beggar had solicited alms of Mohammed, who, apparently having no money with him, had borrowed a drachma of the speaker to give to the beggar. This drachma Mohammed had omitted to return to him. Such, we are told, was the slight record of wrong and indebtedness of the founder of a religion which hundreds, aye thousands, of millions of human beings have professed in life and have adhered to until their last breath.

CHAPTER XV

CONCLUSION

Truths can never be confirmed enough,

Though doubts did ever sleep.

SHAKESPEARE

ENGLISHMEN who are old enough to remember the Crimean war might well rub their eyes on coming to Constantinople to-day, where the stranger, after being shown the public fountain in Stamboul dedicated by the German Emperor to the Sultan, is taken over the water to Scutari, where, in the most picturesque cemetery in the world, England's dead warriors sleep under the cool shade of the cypress-tree. Gone are the days when Englishmen and Turks fought as Allies, when the Sultan Abdul Medjid visited the British Embassy as the guest of his trusted friend, Lord Stratford de Redcliffe, when English capitalists supported Turkey's credit, and English merchant princes first introduced railways into Turkey and dominated the sea-borne commerce as well as the passenger traffic of the Levant. In those times the Englishman embodied in the eyes of the Mohammedan Turk all that was estimable and reliable among the "Franks."

Since those comparatively recent days many changes have been wrought. Foreign bankers, powerful international syndicates have encroached upon English financial influence, and nearly all the Turkish railways and most of the shipping have gone into other than English hands. The finest passenger steamers that come to Constantinople are German, Austrian, Italian, and Russian. The dead alone sleep on as before, under the shady groves of Scutari.

Whatever may be the causes which have brought about these changes, it is permissible for an Englishman to deplore them, not only on economic grounds, but also as a matter of sentiment and of sympathy with the Turks, who have been the greatest losers thereby.

Alas that the supreme ordainment of things in the life of nations, even of whole races and creeds, takes small account of the ups and downs, the sufferings of whole generations of human beings, whatever be their virtues. The Albigenses represented a far higher level of culture, conduct, and principle than those who took up arms against them and brought about their extermination. So also with regard to the Turks in our day, their good qualities are not those which are imperative in order to enable a community to hold its own in times of strenuous commercialism and of unscrupulous political rivalry and intrigue.

For many years the traveller entering Turkish territory at the railway station of Mustapha Pasha saw the Custom House officers in ragged uniforms, on the look-out for baksheesh, since their small salary, if ever paid, was certainly in arrear. How could he come to any other conclusion than that conditions prevailed here which are no longer tolerable in Europe? For even in Asiatic Russia, with all its backwardness, they do not exist. This impression of the anachronism of a Turkey in Europe is likely to be applied to Asia as well by those who have traversed that part of the world, unless some drastic administrative and financial reforms are put into force at once.

Calling one day in the summer of 1896 at the British Embassy, at Therapia, the late Sir Michael Herbert, who was in charge during Sir Philip Currie's absence, told me that about a hundred years ago the Ambassador of the French Republic at Constantinople, in writing home to his Government, wound up his letter by declaring that the prospects of Turkey looked so desperate that he would not be surprised if the Turkish Empire had ceased to exist before the arrival of his letter.

During a visit I paid to Constantinople in January 1907 something occurred which impressed me forcibly with the conviction that the Hamidian régime, the desire of one man, however well-intentioned and industrious, to do single-handed all the directing work of an empire, was doomed to failure; and this in spite of the many evidences I had had, both in Europe and in Asia, of the personal popularity of the Sultan. It was the talk of Pera that the Chief of the Secret Police, Fehim Pasha, had been guilty of some extraordinary pranks; among them the instigation of sham conspiracies which he pretended to nip in the bud in order to give proof of his devotion to the Sultan. All attempts to draw the Sultan's attention to this man's misdeeds had apparently failed, owing, it was said, to His Majesty's indulgence towards one who was the son of his own foster-brother. Emboldened by success, Fehim Pasha had extended his sphere of black-mailing operations to members of the European colony, while several murders were put to his account as having been their instigator. Still he managed to elude the arm of justice. At last he took upon himself to lay an embargo on a ship, either belonging to a German or in the cargo of which some German firm was interested. Here, however, he came into conflict with the German Ambassador, the late Baron Marschall von Bieberstein, who promptly took the part of his countrymen, saw that the embargo on the ship in question was removed, and, distrustful of the dilatoriness of the officials at the Sublime Porte, lodged a strongly worded complaint direct at the Palace. This ultimately resulted in Fehim Pasha being banished to Asia Minor, where he was subsequently assassinated by a mob in the street. This tragic development, however, only took place after I had left Constantinople.

The German Ambassador, who was always very friendly and frank with me, one day discussed the situation created by Fehim Pasha's delinquencies. He convinced me that the man was a scoundrel, and that he himself had done no more than what he was perfectly entitled to do in endeavouring to bring one to book who was neither more nor less than a criminal miscreant, fully deserving to be given over to the public hangman.

I happened to call at the Palace next day, and went up as usual into the private room of Izzet Pasha, where, quite unexpectedly, I met my old friend Ahmed Midhat Effendi. It was one of the very few times I had ever known him to pay a visit to the Palace. Fehim Pasha's crimes and the energetic measures of the German Ambassador formed the subject of conversation in the room. Izzet Pasha warmly expressed his indignation at an Ambassador presuming to interfere in what he considered to be a purely internal incident. "Qu'est ce qu'il s'imagine, ce Monsieur de Marschall?" Knowing what I did of the affair on such good authority, I was taken by surprise, the more so as Ahmed Midhat Effendi joined in upholding the innocence of the incriminated pasha. I could scarcely credit the culpable ignorance thus revealed to me by those to whom it should have been a first care not to lead their master astray on an issue of such vital importance. I said it was hopeless for the well-wishers of Turkey to attempt to say a good word for their Government as long as such things were possible; that the German Ambassador had had the training of a State Prosecutor, and certainly was not one to be misled by unreliable evidence, or to be moved from his point once he had decided upon it; and that English newspapers, which were not usually over-favourably disposed to German interests, had strongly supported the Ambassador in this particular matter. But it was all to no purpose. I failed to shake their belief in Fehim Pasha's innocence. They even asserted that he was quite a good fellow. The most they would admit was that he had been somewhat hasty and headstrong owing to his youth, "un peu étourdi." It is only fair to state, however, that those present did not show any ill-feeling at my being so plain-spoken; but this was only in accordance with what I have so often experienced in the Turkish character. Still I left the Palace with a pessimistic feeling.

Sirry Bey, who had been the chief of our expedition in Armenia, called on me at the Pera Palace Hotel one evening and said: "I come to you on behalf of His Majesty. He feels his dignity trespassed upon by the interference of the German Ambassador in this Fehim Pasha business, which he holds to be one of an internal nature not concerning a foreign Ambassador, and he would like to see you." I mentioned to Sirry Bey what I had heard from the Ambassador, and told him that it seemed to me to be a black business, and he would do well to convey this opinion to the Sultan. In due course I received a message to come up to the Palace immediately as the Sultan wanted to see me.

On my arrival I was taken in to His Majesty, and he at once began to discuss the Fehim Pasha incident, and to complain of the conduct of the German Ambassador. As the editor of the *Daily Mail* had asked me to send him a report in case I should have an opportunity of interviewing the Sultan, I asked His Majesty whether he would wish me to give his version of the affair to that paper, at the same time repeating to him what I had heard about Fehim Pasha's delinquencies. Whether the Sultan attached any importance to what I told the interpreter I am unable to say, but in reference to my suggestion he held up his hands in a deprecatory manner, and uttered the words, "Yok! yok!" ("No! no!") twice in succession.

"It is nothing more than my plain duty to see justice done," the Sultan said to me. And as if it were monstrous that a doubt could exist with regard to so self-evident a truism, he added: "Even if it were one of my own sons, I would see justice done."

Of course, I respected his wishes, and did not refer at all to the German Ambassador in my interview with His Majesty, a report of which appeared in the *Daily Mail* of March 8, 1907. There would also have been no point in my doing so, as I was convinced of the hopelessness of the Sultan's case, whatever might have been the uncompromising attitude the German Ambassador had taken up. Since such outrages were possible under the very eyes of the diplomatic representatives of the Great Powers in the capital in broad day, was it not within the range of probability that many crimes which had been imputed to the Sultan had indeed been committed, though without his knowledge? I left Constantinople with the conviction that nothing, not even the support of the German Empire, could long sustain a régime in which such things were allowed to happen.

The rivalry of the different European nationalities forms too important a feature in the eyes of the foreign visitor, at least those of a political turn, not to call for comment. Nowhere are Goethe's words—written nearly a hundred years ago—more applicable than to this subject:

Und wer franzet oder brittet,

Italienert oder teutschet

Einer will nur wie der Andere

Was die Eigenliebe heischet.

West-Oestlicher Divan

The idea conveyed is that whether a man speaks in the name of France, Britain, Italy, or Germany, the burden of his contention is invariably self-interest, self-love.

The question of German influence in Turkey has become such a prominent feature in the public eye that it seems to warrant more than a passing reference from one who has had many opportunities of following its development. Our attention has been drawn so much of late to this influence that we are apt to lose sight of what is likely to be a more lasting, as it is certainly a more valuable, feature, namely, its effect as a practical civilizing force. Indeed, this advent of the German, and with him of the Belgian, the Swiss, the Italian, and the Hungarian, as financial and industrial pioneers, as erectors of railways, schools, hospitals, and other useful institutions, may be said to mark a new beneficial era in the East. Nor should it be forgotten that the Germans and their partners have now and then shown a commendable spirit in inviting the co-operation of others whom they to some extent have superseded. For although the Anatolian Railway is essentially a German undertaking, M. Huguenin, a French Swiss, has been elected its chairman. The Mersina-Adana Railway, originally an English enterprise, has also been taken over by the Germans, but they have re-elected the former chairman, an Englishman, resident in Constantinople, to preside over the board of directors. Nor need there be any reason why, under normal conditions, a similar friendly co-operation should not exist in all directions, not merely in commercial and financial matters, but also in the domain of politics. It is therefore to be regretted that the flamboyant circumstances under which the Sultan's Iradè for the concession of the Bagdad Railway was obtained, and suddenly communicated to the world by the usual telegram, were calculated to arouse an uneasiness in the public mind which a less sensational departure would have avoided. The onerous financial guarantees imposed upon the Turkish Government by the German concessionnaires have not tended to increase the popularity of the German element among thoughtful Turks or the broad strata of the Turkish people who are called upon to make sacrifices for an undertaking the political and economic importance of which they have not the knowledge to appreciate. To such as these the German concessionnaire appears somewhat in the light of the usurer, who is now in addition credited with political aims which Germany long persistently repudiated. But however this may be, there can be little doubt that she has lost rather than gained in her hold on the sympathies of the Turks, since, in addition to the scalpel of the surgeon, the text-book of the schoolmaster, and the staff of Mercury, she has added the sword of the soldier and the Field-Marshal's baton to the emblems of her activities in the Ottoman Empire, and increased the jealousy of the other Great Powers. Promises of political support to Turkey were undoubtedly given. The Sultan was encouraged to favour the reactionary military element in making appointments. Soldiers were asked for as Ambassadors in preference to diplomatists of Phanariote families, although the latter had supplied for generations past the most able Turkish diplomatists. By Imperial desire a Mohammedan Turkish cavalry officer, Tewfik Pasha, a charming companion, but one completely ignorant of politics, was appointed Turkish Ambassador in Berlin, and remained there until the Turkish revolution in 1908. It is not for non-Germans to decide whether it was to the advantage of the more solid German interests in Turkey and of Turkey herself that the Sultan's favourites were loaded with Prussian decorations. The last Grand Vizier of Abdul Hamid, Ferid Pasha, an Albanian, only a few days before his dismissal received the Grand Cross of the Black Eagle, a distinction supposed to be on a level with our Order of the Garter. There are things a Government can do which would be reprehensible if done by a private individual, but there are also things which are permissible to an individual but which a Government cannot do without imperilling those unweighable assets the correct estimation and cherishing of which was one of Bismarck's strongest points. He would never have stooped to such little manœuvres; neither have the English nor the Russians nor even the French condescended to curry favour with the Turks by such questionable means.

For years past the German official world has made a business of flattering the Turks, instead of warning them and, as true friends, insisting on the execution of the reforms upon which the public opinion of Europe insisted. This has been more particularly the case since the Græco-Turkish war of 1897, which was the moment when Germany might have been able to at least postpone the evil day of reckoning which has come in our time on the blood-stained fields of Thrace and Macedonia.

Turkey's German friends, with all the privileged insight they were allowed into her affairs, appear to have been blind to the black political outlook of the Turkish Empire which politically gifted Italians such as Mazzini and Crispi foresaw and confidently foretold half a century ago. Germany's policy in Turkey encouraged the Turks to procrastinate and assume a truculent attitude. Hence the collapse of Turkey has been a moral blow to military Germany which might have been avoided, and which no sophistry can hide.

The Turkish officers who have served in the German army may have become imbued with the militant atmosphere of the officers' mess of the Potsdam Guards; but this does not mean that they have assimilated the better qualities of the German army. And even if they had, they could not possibly hope to engraft these upon the Mohammedan Turk, who is in every way their antithesis. The Turks are very different from the imitative, assimilative Japanese, with whom German military instructors are said to have been so successful. Thus, contrary to current surmise, I venture to hold the heretical opinion that the expectations founded in some quarters on a successful

Germanization of the Turkish army are doomed to disappointment. The best type of English or French officers would be more likely to suit as instructors of the Asiatic Turks, as they have both proved their capacity in this respect in their dealings with Asiatics in the past. But an even more pressing question may possibly present itself, namely, the growing political aspirations of Germany in Turkey, which her policy since Bismarck's retirement, hand in hand with the optimistic publications of many German military writers, has done so much to encourage. These elements also find a support to-day in the headstrong aggressiveness of the Turkish officers above referred to. According to a recent interview with the King of Roumania, that far-sighted monarch characterized them as the one danger still threatening peace in the East.

The English, whatever their mistakes may have been, have played a more dignified and, as I venture to believe, a more far-sighted part—one which thoughtful Turks now recognize was well meant to Turkey.

The general policy of England is graphically laid down in the following letter which the late British Ambassador at Constantinople, Sir Nicholas O'Conor, favoured me with a few months before his death:

"I have no hesitation in saying that I think the strong point in our English policy is the fact that we have invariably based our representations to the Ottoman Government on the undoubted interests of both the Christian and Moslem subjects of the Sultan; that we have upheld justice to all the people; and that we have fought for an honest administration and political freedom, without compromising either the interest of the State or its Sovereign.

"We have kept aloof from the many selfish and ruinous commercial concessions which have been so disastrous in their consequences, and we have abstained from any demands which were not in the interests of Turkey as well as of England. We alone have built, organized, and developed a railway without a penny guarantee from the Turkish Government, and by capable and honest administration we have made it a commercial success. I refer, of course, to the Smyrna-Aidin Railway.

"This attitude on our part has been appreciated by Turkey and more especially by the Moslems.

"The several demands which England has put forward as conditions to her consent to the 3 per cent. increased Customs duty are as much in the interests of Turkish as of foreign trade, and our resolute insistence on these points has been an object-lesson all round.

"We have impressed upon Turkey the advantages of developing her enormous internal resources, and we have succeeded in obtaining such alterations of the old Mining Law as will now permit British as well as foreign capital to be embarked in Turkey without more risks than usually attend such enterprises."

My own experience fully corroborates the above statement of the British Ambassador that the Mohammedans have indeed appreciated the rectitude of English policy and its freedom from all shady transactions. Also as regards the best class of Englishmen (for these alone come into consideration)—once they have rid themselves of their prejudices—their self-restraint, reserve, and, above all, their reliability and fair dealing in personal intercourse generally cause them to be trusted, if not liked, by the Mohammedan, who instinctively distrusts effusiveness, voluble protestations, and more particularly the obtrusiveness associated with the pushing commis-voyageur. This explains why many Turks, even in the hour of their humiliation, prefer the English to others in spite of many advantages they may have reaped from the latter.

That Germany may retain and even increase the commercial hold which she has already gained in Turkey seems more than likely unless others are prepared to compete successfully with her in financial enterprise and industrial efficiency. Her geographical position places her in easy connexion with the Turkish Empire for commercial purposes not only through Roumania and the Black Sea but also by the Danube and by rail through Servia and Bulgaria. All this is decidedly in her favour. But whether in the long run she will be able to use these assets to gain a permanent political ascendancy extending over Asia Minor, as openly advocated by the pan-German party, may well be open to question. Certain idiosyncrasies of the German character erect between the races a barrier which does not exist when the Turk comes into contact with the English, the Italians, the French, and the Greeks. Apart from all this the geographical position of Germany seems to set fixed limits to her political ambitions. For if there is a country the situation of which might well entitle her to look forward to political possibilities in Turkey, it is surely Austria-Hungary, whose frontiers for centuries past along the Danube have been co-terminating with those of Turkey. The character of the Austro-Hungarians also shows many points of affinity with that of the Turks. The German language is another stumbling-block in the way of extending German ideas beyond certain limits,[29] and it encounters a powerful competitor in the French language. French has been recognized in Turkey as the foremost tongue of the "Franks" for nearly three hundred years. There are close upon six hundred schools in Turkey in which French forms part of the regular curriculum. French is spoken more or less by nearly every Turkish official above a certain rank; German by scarcely any. This difficulty of the German language competing with the French has already been felt by the German authorities engaged in the working of the Anatolian Railway. It will also be found a hindrance in case serious efforts should be made to start German colonies along the track of the railway, a plan few people who have visited these regions think likely to succeed, at least yet awhile, although many Germans will recall the strange story of the Saxon colony in Transylvania, and fondly imagine that this unique phenomenon is likely to repeat itself in Asia Minor. Germany's geographical position, which is in her favour where commercial facilities are concerned, is decidedly against her once political influences come to the fore. Several instances in point have arisen of late years in which she has been unable to convert her Turkish sympathies into effective action in favour of Turkey against the opposition of Russia, France, and England. This was notably the case in the naval demonstration against Turkish rule in Crete in 1898 and also in a lesser degree in the Græco-Turkish war of 1897, when, Russia objecting to the German military instructors taking part in that campaign, Turkey was prevailed upon to recall those who had already started for the front. An even more recent case in which Germany failed to support Turkish interests successfully arose in connexion with English action on the Egyptian frontier, and this is still in public memory. But by far the most potent cause which is likely to prevent German political influence getting beyond certain well-defined limits in Turkey is to be found in the ever-watchful jealousy of Russia—Turkey's most relentless and stealthy foe.

> 29. During our two months' journey through Armenia in 1897–98 Dr. Hepworth and myself did not come across a single German, nor even one person who spoke German, though in common fairness it must be admitted we did not touch the Anatolian Railway tract, which is, of course, largely a German enterprise. French, English, Italian, and Greek were the European languages spoken.

Neither England, France, nor Russia, as great Mohammedan Powers, can be expected in the long run to view the "conversion" of German influence into the assumption of the part of Protector of Islam with complacency, much less with favour. The fact that the action of these Powers is apparently a passive one for the present would not justify us in assuming that it will permanently remain so.

The real disposer of Turkey—the vulture hovering overhead, ready to swoop down upon her, though restrained for a time by the kindly feelings of the present Emperor Nicholas[30]—is, and always was, Russia: Russia, which has steadily and relentlessly aimed at the destruction of the Mohammedan empire of the Ottomans.

> 30. I have it on good authority that the present Tsar solemnly promised Sultan Abdul Hamid that he would not undertake anything against Turkey in his lifetime. This personal promise has been nullified now that the Sultan has been dethroned.

From the moment England and Russia arrived at an understanding the fate of Turkey in Europe was in jeopardy, and any ambitions which Germany had in Turkey were doomed to sterility. Even to-day their hopelessness is not realized, for the Germans still enjoy the fruits of past prestige, and the Russians, who are not petty where great issues are at stake, have quietly looked on at Hedjas and Bagdad Railway concession-mongering. It will only be when Germany makes any serious attempt to galvanize Asiatic Turkey into life that the Russians will and can cry "Halt!"

Friedrich Bodenstedt—and few better judges of Eastern life could be quoted—writing fifty years ago, has the following: "The Caucasus is the basis of future world-hegemony. Which does not mean that it will come about in a day, nor vanish overnight, but gradually and inevitably, without the befooled nations, proudly conscious of their superior education, having a suspicion of the danger which threatens them. The submission of Shamyl in the east and the exodus of the Circassians in the west of the Caucasus are events of which the Press took hardly any notice at the time, but which future generations will consider to be among the most important happenings of the century."[31]

    31. "Tausend und ein Tag im Orient." Berlin, 1865.

A glance at the map of the Turkish Empire and its frontier separating the territories of the Northern Colossus should be sufficient to bring home to the most casual student the full significance of this passage, and to illuminate M. Nelidow's remark to me in 1896, "We shall never allow others to handle the key of our house," meaning the Bosphorus. But nobody could well traverse Anatolia and witness its desolate condition, without roads or bridges—more backward than Siberia or Manchuria—without realizing that the danger of absorption by Russia is like the sword of Damocles, a menace ever present. As a matter of fact, Russia occupied Erzeroum temporarily in 1878, and only the pressure of England at the Congress of Berlin induced her to withdraw. As long as England was at variance with Russia the danger was kept in suspense, but now that they are united in an entente it would be foolhardiness for any other Power to imagine that it could intervene and prevent by force of arms any consummation which these two had agreed upon. Should such an entente lead to a dividing up of Asiatic Turkey into different spheres of influence among the Great Powers, there would in all probability be a European war, as foreshadowed by Professor Vambéry,[32] which ultimately would be only too likely to result in the incorporation of the greater part of Turkey in Asia in the Russian Empire, since Russia never will, and in view of her geographical position never can, allow Germany to be the permanently dominating influence on the Bosphorus.

    32. See Appendix, p. 291.

In the course of my first visit to Prince Bismarck in April 1891, the topic of Russia's intentions with regard to Constantinople was discussed. To my surprise, the Prince stated that he did not believe Russia intended to take Constantinople. Russia might even undertake to guarantee the Sultan in the possession of his palaces, his harem, and his wives on condition that no other strong Power should be dominant on the Bosphorus. I ventured to ask the Prince whether he did not think such a development might be inimical to British interests. Bismarck replied: "Not necessarily so."[33]

> 33. I was on the point of publishing this conversation at the time, but wrote first to Bismarck to ask his permission, to which he replied asking me to refrain from publication.

Leaving these far-flung possibilities out of consideration, it is worth while pondering what beneficial part England can play in the East. Many liberal-minded Englishmen have advocated that Germany and England should join hands with other nations and endeavour to work peacefully together, in order to enable Turkey to introduce reforms, exploit her unlimited resources, and thus place herself in a strong independent position in Asia; the only hope left to her.

The British Government might be careful not to send minor officials to Turkey imbued with dislike for the Turk. Such men play into the hands of our rivals by drawing up reports marked by ill-feeling towards the Turks, by corresponding with English newspapers in the same vein, and thereby they indirectly hamper English chances in the competition for commercial advantages. When these practices have ceased, then the goodwill of the Turk will come as a matter of course, and will readily take the practical shape of giving English capital an equal chance in competing for the many valuable opportunities for developing trade still to be had in Turkey; for it may come as news to many Englishmen that, next to Holland and Switzerland, Turkey has the lowest tariff of any country in Europe, and approaches nearest to the English ideal of Free Trade. The splendid work already done by England in Egypt, particularly in the matter of irrigation, affords ample guarantee that honest co-operation between England and Germany, as advocated by Lieutenant-Colonel H. P. Picot (see Appendix, p. 294), might not only result in an addition to, but in a multiplication of, forces working for the benefit of Turkey and for the advantage of the world at large.

APPENDIX

IN the autumn of 1912 a paragraph appeared in a London evening paper announcing that a street in Plumstead had been named after Professor Arminius Vambéry, the eminent Hungarian scholar, who, as is well known, was a personal friend of Queen Victoria and Edward VII, and I sent it to him. This little incident led to a correspondence between us, of which the following letters of the Professor, written in English, are a portion. After his death I sent copies to his son, Dr. Rustem Vambéry—who, like his father before him, is now a Professor at the University of Budapest—and received by return the authorization to publish them, which is embodied in the first letter of the series. In view of the eminence of Professor Vambéry as an authority on Eastern affairs, I gladly avail myself of his kind permission to do so.

BUDAPEST, *October 11, 1913*.

DEAR MR. WHITMAN,—I thank you most heartily for the delicacy of feeling which prompted you to give me the opportunity of revising my father's letters to you, which you are quite at liberty to publish.

I have read them carefully through, and see no reason to alter or omit anything. You know how proud my father was of his status as an independent man, who could freely express his views without let or hindrance. Why should I not continue to act for him in this spirit now that he has passed away?

It might perhaps interest you to know that your work on Austria[34] was the last book he read in his life. The afternoon before his death he asked me to read a few pages aloud, for his sufferings (oppression of the heart) were alleviated by the distraction.

He was a great admirer of your writings, a feeling which has been fully inherited by

Yours most sincerely,

DR. R. VAMBÉRY

(Professor of Criminal Law at the University of Budapest).

[34]. "The Realm of the Habsburgs," by Sidney Whitman. Wm. Heinemann, London, 1892.

I

BUDAPEST UNIVERSITY, *November 12, 1912.*

DEAR MR. WHITMAN,—It was very kind of you to remember the old Dervish and to take interest in the honour bestowed upon him by your magnanimous countrymen.[35] Any services I may have rendered to England are insignificant; but I am proud of having been able to champion England's interests, for, in spite of all shortcomings, you are still the greatest nation in the world.

The fate of our poor Turkish friends is sealed. They will get rid of the cumbersome European ballast, and it is to be wished that they should be able to recuperate in Asia, where they cannot be replaced by any other Moslem nation. Their collapse in Europe was inevitable, and it is only the suddenness of the fall which has surprised me.

My son is much pleased by your kindly remembrance of the slight attention he was able to pay to you. He only acted as in duty bound towards a foreigner and an Englishman.[36]

Yours very truly,

A. VAMBÉRY.

> 35. Reference to the naming of a street in Plumstead already mentioned above.
>
> 36. Reference to my stay in Budapest in the summer of 1897, during which I made the acquaintance of Professor Vambéry's son.

II

December 14, 1912.

DEAR MR. WHITMAN,—Allow me to express to you the great pleasure I felt in reading your article published in the *Pall Mall Gazette* under the title "Some German Military Writers."[37] It is certainly highly gratifying that you, sir, whom I know as the most able writer on German affairs in England, should have come forward to give a good lesson to these overbearing gentlemen. It is in any case a most important *signum temporis*, and it must diminish the idolization of brutal force, of sad mediæval traditions. The eminent soldier who wrote the book "Unser Volk in Waffen" (General von der Goltz) is often quoted by Germans when comparisons are drawn between England and Germany's Imperial power, and deductions are drawn therefrom of Britain's near downfall. Well, let us hope that they are grossly mistaken, just as they were mistaken in predicting a sure victory for the poor Turks, of whom a great German once stated, in the presence of Sultan Abdul Hamid, that *"one Turkish soldier was worth three Prussians."* The German military instructor may have succeeded in turning the goodly Turk into a Prussian, minus the Pickelhaube, but Lule-Burgas has proved a most cruel disenchantment to the glorifiers of General Bernhardi's theories.

In so far I agree with your views. But there is one point with regard to which the English must take particular care, and this is not to fall into the mistake of disregarding the necessity arising from the general situation of European armaments. Formerly the English were quite right to pity the man on the Continent forcibly made a soldier; to-day, however, you must consider the Latin saying, *Ulula cum lupis*, and you are compelled to take note of your next-door neighbours. You must approve Lord Roberts's efforts regarding compulsory military service. If Lord Haldane finds it possible to admire all sorts of German theories and institutions, why does he make an exception with regard to universal military service, which is a genuine German invention?

Yours very truly,

A. VAMBÉRY.

<u>37</u>. In the issue of December 4, 1912.

III

BUDAPEST UNIVERSITY, *December 30, 1912.*

DEAR MR. WHITMAN,—I have read your ably written chapter on Sultan Abdul Hamid with much interest, and I may tell you that I can neither add to nor take away anything from its contents. Of course there is a good deal I could say about the man whose favourite I was supposed to be during more than ten years, but it is impossible to lift the veil more than I did in the two essays I published in the June and July numbers of 1909 of the *Nineteenth Century and After*, in which you can find more than one episode worth reproduction.

Abdul Hamid was decidedly an extraordinary man. Want of able and trustworthy Ministers caused his downfall; but it is generally admitted that if he had remained on the throne the present catastrophe would not have taken place. As I hear from Constantinople, he has got much chance to return to power. The bulk of the nation is siding with him. The Young Turks confess themselves the mistake they made (*vide* a paper by Husein Djahid, the editor of the *Tanin*, in the January (1913) number of the *Deutsche Revue*). The adherents of the old school were always in the Opposition, but the blow was too heavy a one, and I very much doubt whether he, or anybody else, will be able to heal the wounds.

Be so kind as to let me have a copy of the book you will publish, as I am much interested in the late Sultan. Properly speaking, I was not his favourite, for he wanted to use my pen in the interest of Russia, whereas I endeavoured to turn him into British waters, in which I should have probably succeeded if your politicians and your public opinion had not been under the sway of false humanitarian views, and if your nation had not lost the persistency of bygone ages.

In a personal meeting with you I could furnish you with more than one detail. With best greetings from my son,

Yours sincerely,

A. VAMBÉRY.

IV

January 1, 1913.

DEAR MR. WHITMAN,—My letter of yesterday will answer most of your questions, and I only write to tell you that your friendly feelings towards Sultan Abdul Hamid ought not to blind you to the real character of this unfortunate prince. He was decidedly highly gifted, though this was less apparent towards the end of his reign. He suffered from the defects of Eastern princes and of Orientals in general. His intentions may have been honest, but the means he applied were decidedly perverse and he never listened to advice, nor did he believe in anybody.

At all events I look forward to the issue of your book with interest.

Yours sincerely,

A. VAMBÉRY.

V

January 6, 1913.

DEAR MR. WHITMAN,—I had great pleasure in perusing the copy I duly received of your chapter on Sultan Abdul Hamid. Your able pen has lent colour to his career, even though you could not of course deal fully with his real doings.

If I have not always done full justice to this extraordinary man, I may plead some excuse. For more than twelve years I worked hard, I even risked my life, to lead him into the harbour of political security by which the present catastrophe could have been avoided, without, I regret to say, being able to achieve any result.

His entourage made him over-cautious and distrustful, and I am sure he will be haunted by remorse when he remembers our long evening conversations in the Yildiz Kiosk or Chalet Kiosk. He is not the only culprit: your statesmen, too, have made great mistakes.

I trust your poetical pen will be fully appreciated by the reading public, for, as I have told you already, Abdul Hamid has still a fair chance of coming back to the throne. But I do not envy him on that account. It would only turn out to be a midsummer night's dream.

In reciprocating your good wishes for the New Year,

I beg to remain, yours sincerely,

A. VAMBÉRY.

P.S.—Pray give my compliments to M. Chedo Mijatovich.[38] I am very glad that *Bog dal srecu yunacku*[39] to his countrymen.

> [38]. The distinguished Servian historian and diplomatist, formerly Minister of Finance in Servia and Servian Minister in London, where he has since taken up his residence.

> [39]. "God has given the good luck of heroes."

VI

February 11, 1913.

DEAR MR. WHITMAN,—I delayed answering your last letter as I was awaiting the arrival of the book you promised to send me. Now that your most interesting and fascinatingly written study on Germany[40] has arrived I hasten to express to you my best thanks for the pleasure I have derived from your book, as well as for your kind reference to my Essays on Sultan Abdul Hamid.[41]

In writing about leading contemporaries we are apt to get into a predicament, evidently not unfamiliar to you, which causes us a great deal of trouble. Those who know cannot write and those who write most do not know. At all events the personality of Abdul Hamid is a landmark in the history of the Osmanides which will be often spoken of.

The Persian poet whom I quote at the end of my article on Abdul Hamid is Saadi, and the quotation is derived from the "Gulistan."

Yours sincerely,

A. VAMBÉRY.

> 40. "German Memories." Wm. Heinemann.
>
> 41. *Nineteenth Century and After*, June and July 1909.

VII

February 14, 1913.

DEAR MR. WHITMAN,—Don't take it as a compliment, for it is a fact that during the three days that I was reading, with slight intervals of leisure, your "Deutsche Erinnerungen"[42] all my studies had to take an involuntary pause. Such an extraordinary influence has your masterly pen wrought upon me. I dare say no German would be able to write such a book upon England, although the subject would be most interesting from a national and ethical point of view, considering the liberal views predominating in England and the great achievements of your nation all over the world. I am glad to see that the unjustified enmity between your country and Germany is gradually subsiding. Both nations are supplementary the one to the other, and their mutual friendship furthers the common interests of humanity.

When will your "Turkish Memories" appear? I am anxious to read them.

Yours sincerely,

A. VAMBÉRY.

> 42. German version of my "German Memories". Deutsche Verlagsanstalt, Stuttgart.

VIII

February 20, 1913.

DEAR MR. WHITMAN,—It will give me much pleasure to go through any chapter of your "Turkish Memories" you may choose to send me. Of course one cannot apply a too severe criticism to a writer on Western affairs who is dealing with Eastern topics unless he is under the sway of preconceived notions like Pierre Loti, who, like Lamartine, dips his pen in Castalian fountains. And, besides, Abdul Hamid was to me the most incomprehensible

Oriental character I have met in all my long and variegated Eastern career, and I could not vouch for the correctness of my judgment of him. There is one danger, however, you must take care not to fall into, *i.e.* unconditional Turcophilism. I mean to say you must avoid all sentiment in dealing with politics. Statesmen may have ignored the horrible effects of Turkish misrule and the ruin of the finest portion of Asia, but we writers, at any rate, are bound to speak the truth.

I am no admirer of Sir Edward Grey's policy in the Near East, and still less in Central Asia, but I cannot refrain from calling the German policy haughty and overbearing. Her *Drang nach dem Osten*[43] is silly and childish and must provoke a most bloody contest all over the world. If Germany imitates Austrian methods she will be overtaken by a similar fate, for it is no secret that the sentence, *finis Austriæ*, is looming in the distance.

What I pity is my poor country, whose future is not very bright.

Yours sincerely,

A. VAMBÉRY.

> 43. A current German phrase meaning "The trend towards the East."

IX

February 21, 1913.

DEAR MR. WHITMAN,—I have gone through your manuscript with great pleasure, and all I can say is that indulgence, nobility of mind, gratitude, and gentlemanly feeling form the ruling features of the paper, whereas the manifold harm resulting from the personal idiosyncrasies of the Sultan is only occasionally touched upon.

From your point of view, and judging as a foreigner, you were quite right to use subdued colours, but having acted as a political writer who endeavoured and intended to turn the Sultan on the right way, I am sorry to say I could not follow your example. Nor could any modern Turk who had witnessed the ever-increasing calamity of his country do so. At all events your book will call forth much comment and varied criticism.

Yours sincerely,

A. VAMBÉRY.

X

April 28, 1913.

DEAR MR. WHITMAN,—In reading your well-conceived and well-written book on the "Realm of the Habsburgs" I could not refrain from feeling regret at not having been blessed by nature with that rare gift of literary skill and eminence which distinguishes your pen. Having seen and experienced so much in many countries and in many nations, where I passed as a native, what attractive and truthful pictures could I not have furnished of my variegated experiences, and how considerably I could have facilitated the intercourse between man and man! Well, *non omnes omnia*—and writers like yourself, in whose works I delight, do sometimes darken the distant horizon of my past.

Your book, like the last one I read, is a masterpiece, in spite of the disadvantages resulting from the changes caused by the quick pace of our times, when so many features must obviously alter. It reminds me of an Oriental remark about a decayed beauty: "The mosque has fallen into ruins, but the altar where people worshipped still stands upright." With some slight alterations your book could be advantageously republished. I am exceedingly sorry to be so far from dear old England, for, owing to this distance, many interesting items culled from my daily Turkish, Persian, and Tartar reading are lost to the public. Germany is not the place for practical Eastern topics: a long essay written on the slippers of Goethe is more appreciated there than a detailed description of recent political events in Turkey, Persia, etc. I was certainly not wrong in saying one day to a great German: "Hätte Deutschland weniger Orientalisten aber mehr Orientkenner gehabt, so brauchten sie heute Englands Stellung in Asien nicht mit neidischen Augen zu betrachten."[44]

You are much younger than I am. Perhaps chance will favour me in seeing you one day in this part of the world.

Yours sincerely,

A. VAMBÉRY.

> 44. "If Germany had possessed fewer Orientalists and a greater number of true judges of the East, she need not have regarded England's position in Asia with envious eyes to-day."

I feel I cannot more fitly conclude my "Turkish Memories" than by citing the letter of Lieutenant-Colonel H. P. Picot, already referred to in the Preface:

"On reading the letter written to you on February 14, 1913, by Professor Vambéry, I was greatly interested to find him saying: 'I am glad to see that the unjustified enmity between your country and Germany is gradually subsiding. Both nations are supplementary the one to the other, and their mutual friendship furthers the common interests of humanity.'

"The Professor, I see, agrees with you that 'the real crux of Turkey's political problems is, and always was, Russia'; and, further, that 'the geographical position of Germany seems to set fixed limits to her ambitions.' It was the realization of these factors by Turkish statesmen that gave Germany her opportunity during the later years of Abdul Hamid's Sultanate. The welcome extended to the German Emperor by the Sultan at the time of his visit to Constantinople and the Holy Land was a direct invitation to Germany to interest herself in the development of the Asiatic provinces of Turkey, and thereby to build up a barrier against Russia in Armenia and Mesopotamia. The Sultan saw clearly that if German capital could be employed on a large scale in the development of railways between the capital and Bagdad, and in opening up the Mesopotamian delta by means of irrigation, etc., his country might obtain that political support which had become practically essential for the preservation of the integrity of his Asiatic dominions.

"The same view was doubtless held by Sir William White, H.B.M.'s Ambassador at Constantinople, who, years ago, was of opinion that, in the interests both of Great Britain and of Turkey, it would be well if Germany were encouraged to extend her influence at Constantinople and in the Balkans.

"Abdul Hamid naturally hoped for the political support of Germany in the Balkans as well as in his Asiatic possessions, though he must have been aware of the difficult position Germany, as a Christian Power, would find herself in should the Balkan States make an effort on a sufficiently wide scale to extend their frontiers at Turkey's expense. In such a case, however, he had little or nothing to expect from Great Britain, and even less from Russia. Thus, Germany was a last hope; and though, as events have shown, her support was of little avail when the psychological moment arrived for the long-expected Balkan war, the Sultan's political sagacity has yet to be proved at fault in so far as Asia Minor is concerned. Germany now possesses great interests in Anatolia and Mesopotamia, and if Turkey is ever to build up her Asiatic Empire and regain her position as a Moslem Power, it will only be done with the assistance and co-operation of Germany and Great Britain. It does not follow that because Germany failed Turkey in Europe, she will do so in Asia. The problem is a different one in that quarter, where it has lost its peculiarly European character. It may well be within the power, as it certainly is in the interest, of Great Britain and Germany to safeguard Turkey's sovereign rights in her purely Asiatic possessions. Russia is the enemy at the gate.

"It is of happy augury that the bitterness of feeling that has separated Great Britain and Germany is now fast giving way to a better understanding, and it would be well that Turkish statesmen should realize early in the day that the future of their country depends on welding together, as far as it lies in their power to do so, the economic and political interests of these two countries in Asia. For Russia is already moving in the direction of Mesopotamia and Armenia: her occupation of Persian Azerbaijan, where she has concentrated 17,000 troops, is meant to serve her designs upon Mesopotamia, as the first étape of her advance towards the Persian Gulf.

"Russia has not yet forgotten the lessons of the Russo-Japanese war. If she scents obstacles ahead, she will hesitate to advance too rapidly on the path of adventure. But hesitation is not synonymous with withdrawal. Russia is still true to Gortschakoff's famous phrase, 'La Russie ne boude pas, elle se recueille.' Turkey would be in less danger from her if she could enlist the sympathies and engage the material interests of Great Britain and Germany upon her side, as Abdul Hamid evidently considered that they might be enlisted in regard to his Asiatic dominions.

"As already stated in your own words, 'the geographical position of Germany seems to set fixed limits to her ambitions'; and since Great Britain has no territorial ambitions in Asiatic Turkey—as it is recognized at last, even in Turkey—there is everything to be gained by their loyal and whole-hearted co-operation. But only on such lines.

(Signed) "H. P. PICOT."

Milton Keynes UK
Ingram Content Group UK Ltd.
UKHW042145281024